OECD Studies on SMEs and Entrepreneurship

Policies to Support Green Entrepreneurship

BUILDING A HUB FOR GREEN ENTREPRENEURSHIP IN DENMARK

This document, as well as any data and map included herein, are without prejudice to the status of or sovereignty over any territory, to the delimitation of international frontiers and boundaries and to the name of any territory, city or area.

The statistical data for Israel are supplied by and under the responsibility of the relevant Israeli authorities. The use of such data by the OECD is without prejudice to the status of the Golan Heights, East Jerusalem and Israeli settlements in the West Bank under the terms of international law.

Note by Turkey
The information in this document with reference to "Cyprus" relates to the southern part of the Island. There is no single authority representing both Turkish and Greek Cypriot people on the Island. Turkey recognises the Turkish Republic of Northern Cyprus (TRNC). Until a lasting and equitable solution is found within the context of the United Nations, Turkey shall preserve its position concerning the "Cyprus issue".

Note by all the European Union Member States of the OECD and the European Union
The Republic of Cyprus is recognised by all members of the United Nations with the exception of Turkey. The information in this document relates to the area under the effective control of the Government of the Republic of Cyprus.

Please cite this publication as:
OECD (2022), *Policies to Support Green Entrepreneurship: Building a Hub for Green Entrepreneurship in Denmark*, OECD Studies on SMEs and Entrepreneurship, OECD Publishing, Paris, https://doi.org/10.1787/e92b1946-en.

ISBN 978-92-64-78642-4 (print)
ISBN 978-92-64-56547-0 (pdf)
ISBN 978-92-64-89843-1 (HTML)
ISBN 978-92-64-35455-5 (epub)

OECD Studies on SMEs and Entrepreneurship
ISSN 2078-0982 (print)
ISSN 2078-0990 (online)

Photo credits: Cover © Getty/Nuthawut Somsuk

Corrigenda to publications may be found on line at: www.oecd.org/about/publishing/corrigenda.htm.
© OECD 2022

The use of this work, whether digital or print, is governed by the Terms and Conditions to be found at https://www.oecd.org/termsandconditions.

Foreword

This report offers policy advice to Denmark on building a hub for green entrepreneurship in response to the strategy for Business Promotion in Denmark 2020-23, which calls for efforts to strengthen entrepreneurship, and increase innovation, digitalisation and internationalisation within Danish companies. The policy advice will also support the new panel on green entrepreneurship that has been established by the Danish government.

Mitigating climate change is a critical issue on the global policy agenda. Many governments, and indeed sub-national governments, have committed to ambitious policy targets for moving towards a more green and sustainable economy. Close to 200 parties are signatories to the Paris Agreement to keep the increase in the global average temperature to well below 2 degrees Celsius above pre-industrial levels, with many committing to reach net zero greenhouse gas (GHG) emissions by 2050. These commitments call for rapid innovation and investment to develop new technologies as well as the introduction of new policies that influence the behaviour of people and firms. The COVID-19 pandemic has created an opportunity for governments to advance on this agenda since economic stimulus packages have the potential to support actions that simultaneously achieve environmental objectives. Furthermore, the war in Ukraine and rising energy prices have increased the need for governments to identify new and secure energy sources. The green transition is expected to create opportunities for entrepreneurs to exploit new markets, which will be an important driver for broader change.

The report provides a brief overview of the importance of green entrepreneurship and recent policy actions in OECD countries to stimulate and support green entrepreneurs. It identifies lessons from international policy practices in stimulating and supporting green entrepreneurship from three case study countries – Canada, Germany and Israel – to inform the Danish Business Authority about effective policy practices and pitfalls to avoid as it implements initiatives to strengthen the green transition to meet the objectives of the new strategy for Business Promotion in Denmark 2020-23. The case studies were developed through desk research and interviews with policy officers and green entrepreneurship stakeholders in the case study countries.

This report was presented and discussed at the 2nd session of the Committee on SMEs and Entrepreneurship on 13-14 April 2022. It was approved for publication on for publication on 21 April 2022 [CFE/SME(2022)11].

Acknowledgements

This report was prepared by the Centre for Entrepreneurship, SMEs, Regions and Cities (CFE) of the Organisation for Economic Co-operation and Development (OECD), led by Lamia Kamal-Chaoui, Director, at the request of the Danish Business Authority. It contributes to the programme of work of the OECD Committee on SMEs and Entrepreneurship (CSMEE) on green entrepreneurship and of the OECD Local Employment and Economic Development (LEED) Committee on inclusive entrepreneurship, which is co-funded by the European Commission.

The project was led by David Halabisky, Project co-ordinator, CFE, OECD under the supervision of Jonathan Potter, Head of the Entrepreneurship Policy and Analysis Unit, CFE, OECD and Céline Kauffmann, Head of Entrepreneurship, SME and Tourism Division, CFE, OECD. The report was drafted by a team involving Dr. Pedro Saraiva (NOVA University of Lisbon, University of Coimbra), Pablo Shah (OECD/CFE), David Halabisky (OECD/CFE) and Dr. Luis Viegas Cardoso (University of Oxford). Partners from the Danish Business Authority played a key role in co-ordinating and steering the project, including Torsten Andersen, Simon Hauptmann, Martin Haagensen and Rebekka Edemann.

The OECD team is grateful for the insights provided by policy officers and stakeholders in the three international case study countries: Canada, Germany and Israel. Interviews were held with David Asaf, Head of the Environment and Cleantech Division at the Ministry of Economy and Industry of Israel; Anya Eldan, Head of Startup Division & Business Development at the Israel Innovation Authority; Tyler Hamilton, Director of Ecosystem, Cleantech at MaRS Discovery District in Toronto, Canada; Michael Müllneritsch, Senior Expert in Start-Ups and Innovation at the German Energy Agency (Dena); Dr. Akamitl Quezada, Expert in Energy Efficiency and Energy Services at Dena; David Ryfisch, Team Leader in International Climate Policy at Germanwatch; Matt Stanley, Director at the Cleantech Practice of the Business Development Bank of Canada; and Laura Westhoff, Expert in Energy Transition and Climate Action in Companies at Dena.

Finally, the authors are thankful for the suggestions provided by Nadim Ahmad, Deputy Director of the CFE, OECD; Lucia Cusmano, Deputy Head of Entrepreneurship, SME and Tourism Division, CFE, OECD; Tess Frémont-Côté, Joffre Osborne and Jenifer Pilon of Innovation, Science and Economic Development Canada; and Stephanie Kage and Friederike Morgenstern of the German Federal Ministry for Economic Affairs and Climate Action.

Table of contents

Foreword 3

Acknowledgements 4

Executive summary 8

1 Green entrepreneurship in Denmark: assessment and policy recommendations 11
    Denmark has the potential to be a world leader in green entrepreneurship 13
        Danes are among the most environmentally conscious people in Europe 13
        Denmark has a relative advantage in green innovation 14
        The Danish government has an ambitious climate agenda 15
        Denmark has internationally competitive start-up ecosystems… 17
        …but green start-ups in Denmark face difficulties in scaling up 17
    Current policy approaches to directly promote and support green entrepreneurs 17
        Entrepreneurship financing 18
        Networks 19
        Business support services 19
        Incubators and accelerators 20
        Exporting support 20
        Entrepreneurship education 20
    Building demand for green entrepreneurs' products and solutions 20
        EU-level measures 21
        Danish measures 21
    Policy proposals: building a green entrepreneurship hub 22
      1. Develop a unified green entrepreneurship strategy with periodic monitoring reports 23
      2. Develop a one-stop shop for green entrepreneurship support 24
      3. Support specialised incubators and accelerators that build on local advantages 25
      4. Engage with private sector actors in the design and implementation of programmes 25
      5. Help green entrepreneurs to access global markets 26
      6. Unleash the potential of public procurement as a driver of change 26
      7. Seek to ensure that regulatory frameworks are conducive to green entrepreneurship 26
      8. Harness consumers' environmental concerns to stoke demand for green products 27
      9. Expand green entrepreneurship training and education 27
      10. Foster the development of networks within the green entrepreneurship ecosystem 28
      11. Tailor support programmes to reflect the needs of green entrepreneurs in different sectors and at different stages of development 28
    References 29
    Notes 30

2 The importance of green entrepreneurship — 31
- The need for green entrepreneurship — 32
- Defining green entrepreneurship — 34
- Drivers of green entrepreneurship — 36
- References — 37

3 International policy trends and practices — 41
- Direct supports for green entrepreneurs — 43
  - Supporting the development of green skills — 43
  - Delivering support packages through green incubators and accelerators — 43
  - Facilitating access to green and sustainable finance — 44
  - Using public-private partnership models to create opportunities — 47
  - Increasing diversity in entrepreneurship through green entrepreneurship policy — 48
  - Implementing local public initiatives — 48
  - The role of non-government actors — 49
- Building demand for green solutions — 49
  - Political commitments to shift social attitudes — 49
  - Developing new economic models such as the circular economy — 50
  - Expanding green public procurement — 51
- References — 52

4 Policy approaches to stimulating and supporting green entrepreneurship in Canada, Germany and Israel — 55
- Introduction — 57
- Canada — 57
  - Policy actions that directly support green entrepreneurship — 58
  - Policy actions that indirectly support green entrepreneurship — 62
  - Success factors for stimulating green entrepreneurship — 62
  - Pitfalls and challenges to consider — 63
- Germany — 64
  - Policy actions that directly support green entrepreneurship — 65
  - Policy actions that indirectly support green entrepreneurship — 67
  - Success factors in stimulating green entrepreneurship — 69
  - Pitfalls and challenges to consider — 69
- Israel — 71
  - Policy actions that directly support green entrepreneurship — 71
  - Policy actions that indirectly support green entrepreneurship — 74
  - Success factors in stimulating green entrepreneurship — 75
  - Pitfalls and challenges to consider — 76
- Lessons from Canada, Germany and Israel in promoting green entrepreneurship — 77
  - 1. Integrated governance models tie the system together — 77
  - 2. A "whole business" approach to support green entrepreneurship — 77
  - 3. Green entrepreneurship is about cleantech but not only about cleantech — 77
  - 4. Development of strategic partnerships to advance green entrepreneurship — 78
  - 5. Overcoming funding gaps — 78
  - 6. Green entrepreneurship policies go hand-in-hand with national climate goals — 78
  - 7. Inclusion of under-represented groups — 79
- References — 79
- Notes — 81

Tables

Table 1.1. Summary of policy recommendations and responsible entities 22
Table 2.1. Defining green entrepreneurship 35
Table 4.1. Green entrepreneurship indicators: Denmark vs. Canada, Germany and Israel 57

Figures

Figure 1.1. The majority of Danes list the environment and climate change as being one of the top two issues facing the country 13
Figure 1.2. The share of Danes listing the environment and climate change as being one of the top two issues facing themselves personally is the sixth highest in Europe 14
Figure 1.3. The share of patents in environmental technologies in Denmark is by far the highest in the OECD 15
Figure 1.4. Denmark has moved faster and further than other OECD countries in lowering greenhouse gas emissions 15
Figure 1.5. Falling emissions have not halted economic growth in Denmark 16
Figure 1.6. Environmental taxation as a share of GDP in Denmark is the fourth highest in the OECD 16
Figure 2.1. Global warming by 2100 depends on climate policies 33
Figure 2.2. The environmental economy is growing faster than the overall economy 37
Figure 3.1. There are fewer than 100 climate technology incubators worldwide 44
Figure 3.2. Links between sustainable and green finance 45
Figure 3.3. Sources of funding for climate technologies 46

Boxes

Box 2.1. Green growth and sustainable development 34
Box 2.2. Green entrepreneurship in the Danish context 36
Box 4.1. Example of a leading green start-up in Canada 58
Box 4.2. Example of a leading green start-up in Germany 64
Box 4.3. Example of a leading green start-up in Israel 71

Follow OECD Publications on:

 http://twitter.com/OECD_Pubs
 http://www.facebook.com/OECDPublications
 http://www.linkedin.com/groups/OECD-Publications-4645871
 http://www.youtube.com/oecdilibrary
 http://www.oecd.org/oecddirect/

Executive summary

This report seeks to support Denmark in implementing initiatives to strengthen its green entrepreneurship ecosystem. Lessons are identified and future policy actions are proposed based on an examination of international policy practices for supporting green entrepreneurship, with a particular focus on the approaches used in three case study countries (Canada, Germany and Israel) that are each recognised as leaders in this area and have similar framework conditions to Denmark.

The case for green entrepreneurship

Combatting climate change is of critical importance to maintaining well-being and standards of living across the world in a sustainable manner. Green entrepreneurship can help develop and propagate new technologies, create new markets and drive change in the business sector. Stimulating green entrepreneurship is therefore an important lever that governments can use to drive the transition to a more sustainable economy.

Green entrepreneurship is a term used widely in academic and policy literature but there has yet to be a convergence on a clear definition. This creates difficulties for governments in targeting policy actions. Based on previous OECD work and building on related concepts of cleantech, greentech and climate tech used in Canada, Germany and Israel, this report defines green entrepreneurship as the development and deployment by new start-ups of green products, services and processes, i.e. those that either:

- reduce or prevent any type of environmental damage; or
- emit less pollution and waste, and/or are more resource-efficient than equivalent normal products, services and processes that have the same result. Their primary use, however, is not one of environmental protection.

Using public policy to stimulate and support green entrepreneurship

Governments in OECD countries have introduced a wide range of policies and schemes to stimulate and support green entrepreneurship in recent years. These include measures that directly support green entrepreneurs by, for example, providing dedicated financial instruments and networks or offering training, incubator and accelerator programmes, as well as broader measures that indirectly support green entrepreneurs by building demand for green solutions. These broader measures include creating and expanding green markets (e.g. public procurement) and regulatory changes (e.g. energy efficiency standards), along with high-level political commitments that signal the need to change the way that societies operate to mitigate the risks of climate change. The latter can accelerate changes in business practices and shift consumers' preferences and expectations, adding to existing social pressures for more sustainable products and production processes.

Denmark has numerous programmes and policy measures in place to directly support green entrepreneurs. These include the Danish Export and Investment Fund and Innovation Fund Denmark, which are important sources of funding for green entrepreneurs. Furthermore, the national cluster organisations are helping to embed green entrepreneurs within networks of businesses, researchers, investors and potential customers, while the six regional business hubs enhance entrepreneurs' access to business support services. The demand for green solutions in Denmark is bolstered by national and European Union-level legislation as well as high levels of public concern about environmental challenges.

The policy approaches and experiences in the case study countries reveal a number of lessons for Denmark. Among these is the need to adopt an integrated governance model, since policies to support green entrepreneurship are initiated by national and sub-national governments and are often launched in partnership with private sector actors. This approach can be seen in Israel, where programmes often involve collaboration between the Israel Innovation Authority, government ministries and the private sector. It is also important for governments to provide a "whole business" approach to supporting green entrepreneurship, since green entrepreneurs need support in a variety of areas including from managing intellectual property to obtaining finance. An example of this can be found in Canada, where the Business Development Bank of Canada utilises a segment-based approach that provides tailored support to entrepreneurs depending on the businesses' size and growth trajectory. Furthermore, the governments in the case study countries take a strong role in helping green entrepreneurs to develop strategic partnerships to commercialise new technologies and practices.

The path forward for Denmark

Denmark has strong foundations for establishing itself as a green entrepreneurship hub. It has set one of the world's most ambitious climate agendas and has moved faster and further than most OECD countries in decarbonising its economy. Support for green entrepreneurship is also strong in Denmark, with an excellent research base and conducive policy framework. Despite this, green entrepreneurs face many obstacles, particularly in scaling up, due to factors such as insufficient access to finance and small domestic markets. Priority actions for strengthening green entrepreneurship policy are:

1. *Develop a unified green entrepreneurship strategy*. Many diverse actors – national and local government, private sector and non-government organisations – support green entrepreneurship in Denmark. However, each operates independently with a distinct set of priorities and objectives, which limits the degree of co-ordination and coherence across green entrepreneurship policies and programmes. A unified strategy would help ensure that relevant entities are working towards common objectives and provide guidance to the many actors for whom green entrepreneurship support is only one of many activities. The Pan-Canadian Framework on Clean Growth and Climate Change can be a model. A core element would be to include a green entrepreneurship data strategy to monitor progress and inform future policy development.

2. *Introduce a one-stop shop for green entrepreneurship support*. Denmark's six regional hubs, together with the *Virksomhedsguiden* portal, operate as a one-stop shop for entrepreneurs and SMEs. There is a clear demand for these services, with the portal receiving 1.1 million website visits in 2021. These services could go further in signposting green entrepreneurship support, making a clear distinction between developing new green solutions and implementing existing green solutions. A good starting point would therefore be to create a dedicated page for green entrepreneurs on the *Virksomhedsguiden* portal that targets entrepreneurs with innovative green solutions looking to bring these ideas to market.

3. *Increase support for specialised incubators and accelerators that build on local advantages*. Business incubators and accelerators play an important role in stimulating the emergence and growth of new enterprises. It will be important to introduce more dedicated programmes for green entrepreneurs within existing incubators and accelerators such as Beyond Beta's Energy Incubator, making sure to build on areas where Denmark has a comparative advantage such as offshore wind and energy efficiency technologies. Inspiration could be drawn from Israel's approach to creating theme-based incubators by selecting and funding private organisations to manage the incubators through a competitive tender process.

1 Green entrepreneurship in Denmark: assessment and policy recommendations

Denmark has the foundations to build a robust and fruitful green entrepreneurship ecosystem, namely an environmentally-conscious population, a world-leading research base in environmental fields, an ambitious climate agenda and a proven track record in lowering greenhouse gas emissions. These foundations are bolstered by the plethora of policy instruments that are available to support the formation and growth of green entrepreneurial ventures through the provision of loans, grants and investment, access to networks and a range of other measures. Despite this potential, Denmark lags behind other OECD countries in certain areas, most notably in the relative shortage of green entrepreneurs that successfully scale up. This chapter provides an overview of green entrepreneurship in Denmark, examining the opportunities, challenges and policy landscape and proposes policy actions to strengthen support for green entrepreneurship.

Highlights

Foundations for boosting green entrepreneurship

- Data from the European Commission's Eurobarometer survey show that the environment and climate change is the most pressing issue for the Danish public, with 51% listing it as being among the top two issues facing the country. This compares to 33% that identified health and 20% that identified the economic situation in Denmark.
- Environment-related technologies accounted for 24% of Danish patents in 2018, which is the highest share in the OECD. This illustrates the relative advantage that Denmark has in green technologies, underpinned by its world-leading research in fields such as energy.
- Denmark has moved faster and further than other OECD countries in reducing its greenhouse gas emissions. In 2020, CO_2 emissions in Denmark were 50% below their 1990 level.

Current state of green entrepreneurship ecosystem

- While Denmark is an established global player in green entrepreneurship, it is not yet a leading hub. In Startup Genome's 2022 rankings, 12 cleantech start-up ecosystems in Europe rank higher than Copenhagen, including three in Scandinavia.
- Start-ups in the environmental technology sector account for a larger than average share of employment, while scale-ups in the sector account for a below average share. This suggests that green start-ups in Denmark face particular difficulties in scaling up.
- Insufficient access to funding appears to be inhibiting the growth of Danish green start-ups. Denmark's venture capital market is small relative to other European countries such as the UK or Sweden, which limits the degree of investment compartmentalisation.

Green entrepreneurship policy landscape

- Finance for green entrepreneurship is supported by a range of dedicated funding instruments that are available through public entities, including the Danish Green Investment Fund, the Danish Growth Fund, Innovation Fund Denmark and a number of development and demonstration programmes.
- National cluster organisations such as Energy Cluster Denmark and CLEAN work to build a bridge between Denmark's research and business communities.
- Denmark has in place a wide range of further support measures that target entrepreneurs more generally. Among these are the six regional business hubs, the *Virksomhedsguiden* portal and Denmark's network of incubators and accelerators, including Beyond Beta.

Core policy recommendations

- Develop a unified green entrepreneurship strategy to align the public and private actors engaged in supporting green entrepreneurship. It would be important to include a green entrepreneurship data strategy to monitor progress and inform future policy development.
- Develop a one-stop shop for green entrepreneurship support to increase visibility of available services.
- Increase support for specialised incubators and accelerators, including the introduction of dedicated programmes for green entrepreneurs within existing incubators and accelerators.

Denmark has the potential to be a world leader in green entrepreneurship

Denmark's green entrepreneurship landscape is ripe with opportunity. In general, a strong green entrepreneurship ecosystem relies upon:

- A strong demand for green goods and services;
- The availability of the skills, infrastructure and technology necessary to develop green products, and;
- A policy framework that supports entrepreneurs in developing green products and converting these innovations into viable and scalable businesses, for instance by promoting access to finance, facilities or training.

In a number of these areas, Denmark stands out as having particularly strong foundations for a thriving green entrepreneurship ecosystem.

Danes are among the most environmentally conscious people in Europe

Opportunities for green entrepreneurs are often underpinned by consumer demand for green goods and services. Therefore, public attitudes towards the environment can influence the health of a green entrepreneurship ecosystem when these environmental concerns translate into a demand for green products. In the Spring 2021 iteration of the European Commission's Eurobarometer, 51% of Danes listed the environment and climate change as being among the top two most important issues facing the country (European Commission, 2021[1]). This is the highest share in the European Union (EU) and the second highest share out of the 41 countries covered by the Eurobarometer (Figure 1.1).

Figure 1.1. The majority of Danes list the environment and climate change as being one of the top two issues facing the country

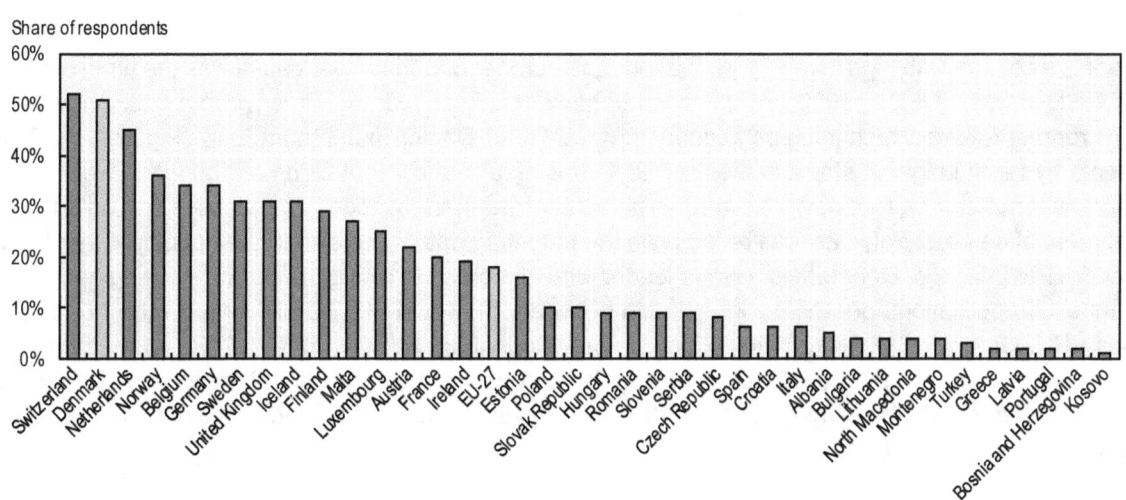

Source: (European Commission, 2021[1])

StatLink https://stat.link/lgxd7m

Danes are also concerned about environmental matters on a personal level. Indeed, more than one-quarter (26%) of respondents cited the environment and climate change as being one of the two most important issues facing them personally (Figure 1.2). Health was the only area that was of greater concern to Danes on a personal level.

Figure 1.2. The share of Danes listing the environment and climate change as being one of the top two issues facing themselves personally is the sixth highest in Europe

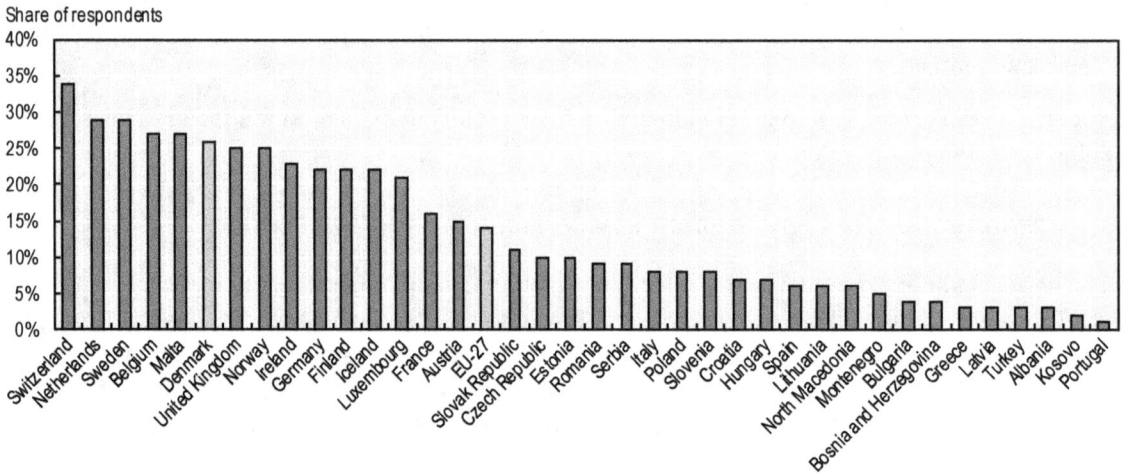

Source: (European Commission, 2021[1])

StatLink https://stat.link/pa1k0b

Denmark has a relative advantage in green innovation

Denmark is a country with high levels of innovation. The number of patents per capita was the ninth highest in the OECD in 2017 (OECD, 2022[2]) and Denmark has a relative advantage in environmental innovation, with environment-related technologies accounting for 24% of Danish patents in 2018 (Figure 1.3). This represents by far the highest share in the OECD. These results show that Denmark punches well above its weight when it comes to innovation and, in particular, green innovation. This applies not only to the development of new technologies – as reflected in the patenting data – but also to the development of new knowledge. For instance, Denmark is a world leader when it comes to energy research, ranking second in the number of publications per million inhabitants between 2013 and 2017 and fourth on the number of citations (IRIS Group & CLEAN, 2019[3]). Furthermore, Copenhagen is part of the STRING megaregion, which has been identified by the OECD as having the potential to become an internationally recognised green hub by virtue of its existing green expertise, high levels of innovation and ambitious infrastructure development plans (OECD, 2021[4]).

Figure 1.3. The share of patents in environmental technologies in Denmark is by far the highest in the OECD

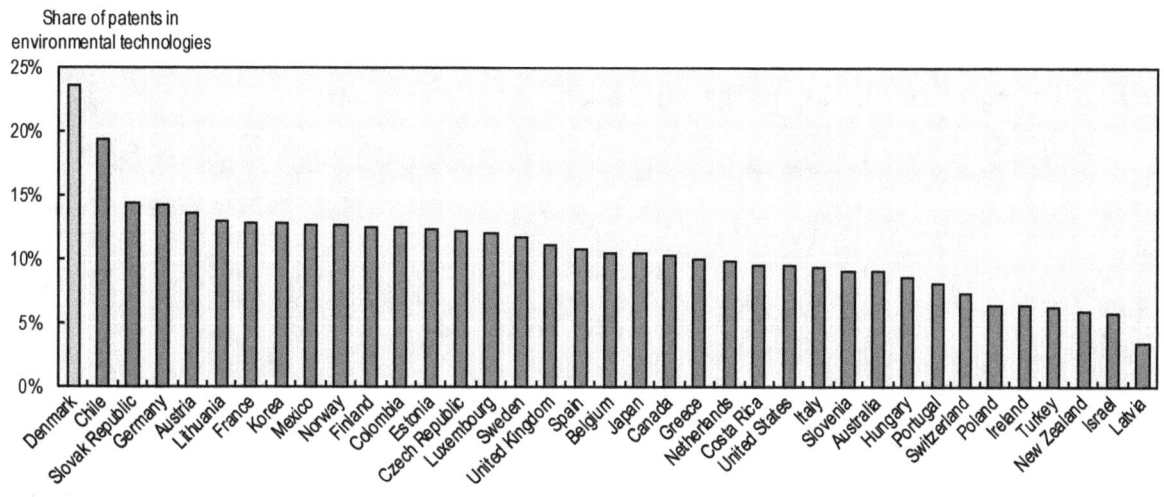

Source: (OECD, 2022[5])

StatLink https://stat.link/m6yoh9

The Danish government has an ambitious climate agenda

Denmark's Climate Act aims to ensure that Denmark lowers its greenhouse gas emissions by 70% below 1990 levels by 2030. This goes over and above the EU's target of lowering greenhouse gas emissions by 55% over the same period. In recent decades, Denmark has made firm progress in shrinking the size of its carbon footprint (Figure 1.4). In 2020, CO_2 emissions in Denmark were already 50% below their 1990 level. By contrast, across the OECD as a whole, CO_2 emissions in 2020 were just 6% lower than in 1990. Therefore, Denmark has a strong head start over other countries on the path towards net zero.

Figure 1.4. Denmark has moved faster and further than other OECD countries in lowering greenhouse gas emissions

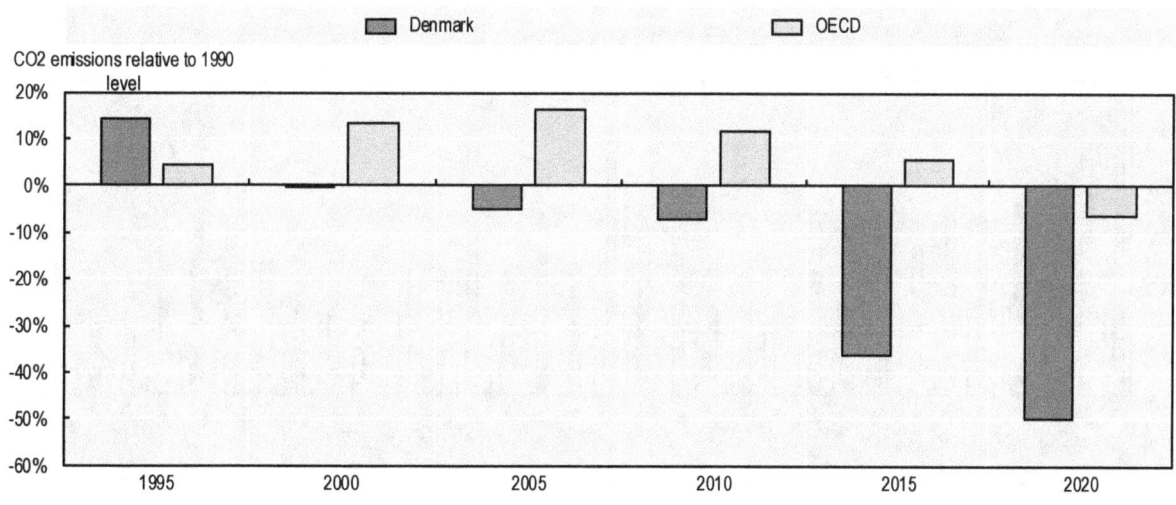

Source: (International Energy Agency, 2022[6])

StatLink https://stat.link/r4jyp6

POLICIES TO SUPPORT GREEN ENTREPRENEURSHIP © OECD 2022

The performance of the Danish economy over the past two decades suggests that the reduction of emissions has not come at the expense of economic growth. Indeed, Denmark's real GDP increased by 25% between 2000 and 2020 (Figure 1.5). During the same period, Denmark's CO_2 emissions were halved.[1]

Figure 1.5. Falling emissions have not halted economic growth in Denmark

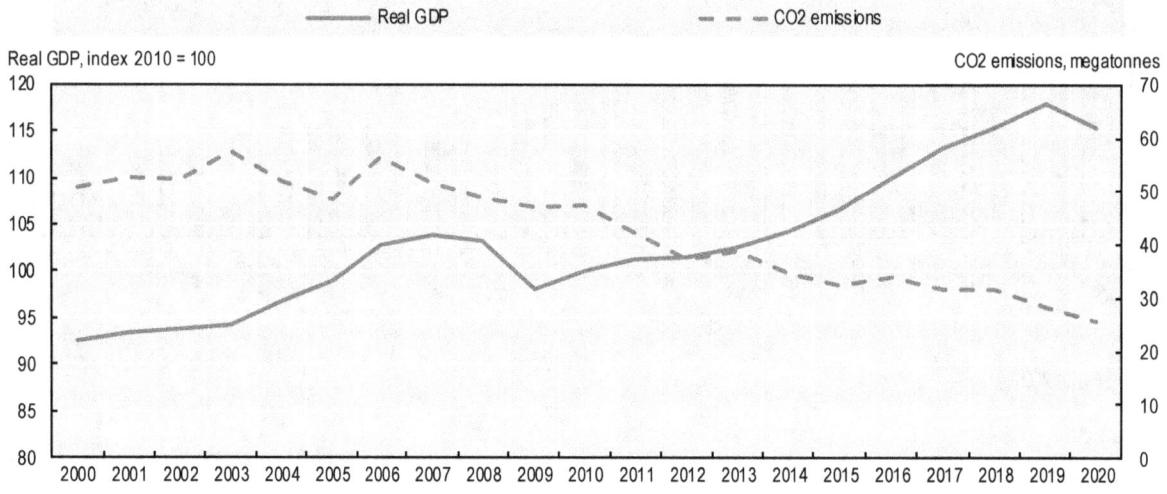

Source: (International Energy Agency, 2022[6]), (Eurostat, 2022[7])

StatLink https://stat.link/rs2u65

Denmark's climate commitments are backed up by a tax regime which, relative to other OECD countries, places a high penalty on polluting activities. Environmental taxes can make it easier for green entrepreneurs to establish a market share by providing green products with a competitive advantage over more polluting alternatives. In 2019, the value of environmental taxes equated to 3.4% of Denmark's GDP (Figure 1.6). Within the OECD, this figure was surpassed only in Estonia, the Netherlands and Slovenia.

Figure 1.6. Environmental taxation as a share of GDP in Denmark is the fourth highest in the OECD

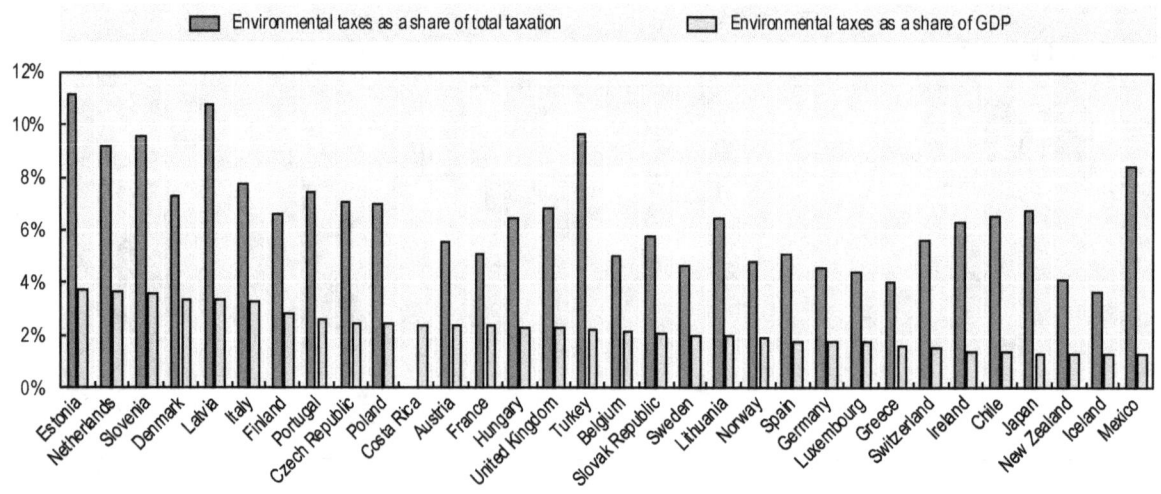

Source: (OECD, 2022[8])

StatLink https://stat.link/xv40r2

Denmark's green entrepreneurship ecosystem has not yet broken through as a leader on the world stage

Denmark has internationally competitive start-up ecosystems…

The level of public support, political will and technological innovation in Denmark implies that the country has the potential to build a world leading green entrepreneurship ecosystem. Strengths have been identified in areas such as wind technology, water technology, energy efficiency and environmental technologies including pollution mitigation and waste reduction (Ministry of Industry, 2021[9]) (Escalona, 2021[10]). However, at present, the evidence suggests that Denmark has not quite reached a leading position in terms of its green entrepreneurship ecosystems.

Copenhagen is placed among the world's 31st - 35th leading cleantech start-up ecosystems in Startup Genome's global 2022 rankings (Startup Genome, 2022[11]). Within Europe, 12 cleantech start-up ecosystems ranked higher than Copenhagen, including three that are located in Scandinavia. The gap in the rankings between Copenhagen and Stockholm – which is Europe's top ranked cleantech start-up ecosystem – is driven principally by significant differences in the number of successful start-ups and funding deals. Startup Genome's analysis finds that the relative strengths of Copenhagen's start-up ecosystem are its research output and level of technological sophistication.

…but green start-ups in Denmark face difficulties in scaling up

Green start-ups account for an above-average share of employment but green scale-ups account for a below-average share. According to data provided by Statistics Denmark, start-ups (i.e. firms aged five years old or younger) in the environmental technology sector accounted for 15% of total employment in the sector in 2019. This compares to a figure of 14% for the business economy as a whole. However, scale-ups (i.e. firms that experienced an annualised growth rate in either employment or turnover of at least 10% over a three-year period having started the period with at least 10 employees) in the environmental technology sector accounted for 19% of employment. This is below the economy-wide average figure of 22%. The fact that start-ups in environmental technology have a larger than average employment footprint while scale-ups in the sector have a below average footprint suggest that green start-ups in Denmark face particular difficulties in scaling up. Indeed, many of the green start-ups featured in TechBBQ's Impact Series identified scaling up as a key challenge. Other issues that were frequently raised are persuading existing industries to embrace change and communicating with potential customers (TECH BBQ, 2022[12]).

Insufficient access to funding may be inhibiting the growth of green start-ups. Denmark's venture capital market is small relative to other European countries such as the UK or Sweden, which limits the degree of investment compartmentalisation (Escalona, 2021[10]). This implies a reduced prevalence of industry-specific venture capital funds, which may inhibit the level of financing received by green start-ups in Denmark. Indeed, TechBBQ's analysis of data from the Danish Venture Capital and Private Equity Association finds that just 7% of venture capital investments in Denmark between 2016 and 2020 were directed towards the cleantech sector, with the majority occurring in the ICT or life science sectors (Escalona, 2021[10]). Investments in green start-ups often require more time to recoup. Also, the societal value of green start-ups' activities is not always fully captured by the financial metrics that are of most interest to traditional investors.

Current policy approaches to directly promote and support green entrepreneurs

Denmark has a range of dedicated policy measures to support green entrepreneurs by providing access to finance, networks, business support services, export promotion, incubation and acceleration, and entrepreneurship education. The legal and regulatory framework also supports green entrepreneurs by raising the demand for green products and solutions. The remainder of this section describes the key policy initiatives that are in place to support green entrepreneurs in Denmark, covering measures at both the domestic and EU-level.

Entrepreneurship financing

Green entrepreneurs in Denmark have the opportunity to tap into a number of public funding sources. The Danish Growth Fund seeks to fill financing gaps left by the private sector by providing a range of financing support measures to entrepreneurs including loans, convertible loans, loan guarantees and direct equity investments. As part of the Danish Green Future Fund, which is a DKK 25 billion commitment designed to support the green transition, DKK 4 billion has been directed to the Danish Growth Fund to finance green businesses in Denmark.

In partnership with financial institutions, the Danish Green Investment Fund lends up to 60% of the costs of environmentally beneficial projects in the areas of energy, food and agriculture, buildings and infrastructure, materials and resources, and transport and mobility. It provides loans of up to DKK 400 million, with a maturity of up to 30 years. The state guaranteed lending limit for the Danish Green Investment Fund was lifted from DKK 2 billion to DKK 8 billion as part of the Danish Green Future Fund. In 2020, the value of outstanding loans issued by the fund stood at DKK 1 649 million. It should be noted that support is available to companies of all sizes, meaning that this initiative does not specifically target entrepreneurs.

As part of the 2022 Agreement on Strong and Innovative Companies, the Danish Growth Fund, Export Credit Agency (EKF) and Danish Green Investment Fund will gradually be merged into a single fund: the Danish Export and Investment Fund. The rationale for the merger is to facilitate synergies between the different funding entities and to make it easier for the design of government funding opportunities to adapt to international developments in a coherent manner. A focus of the Danish Export and Investment Fund will be to strengthen the green transition, which will entail support for green entrepreneurs.

Grants are made available to green entrepreneurs through Innovation Fund Denmark, which is a public investment fund that supports entrepreneurs, businesses and researchers with the potential to develop solutions to societal challenges. Investments are evaluated based on social welfare and environmental factors in addition to financial results, and there is a focus on supporting high risk and high potential projects that may have otherwise found it difficult to obtain finance. One of the three areas that the fund prioritises is climate, environment and green change. In the agreement on the 2021 research reserve, DKK 1.2 billion of investment was assigned to the Innovation Fund to invest in green research initiatives.

Denmark has in place a number of technology development and demonstration programmes, which are an important source of funding for entrepreneurs looking to develop innovative technologies. The Danish Ministry of the Environment oversees the Environmental Technology Development and Demonstration Programme. In 2021, DKK 140 million was made available to companies, research institutions or individuals for the development of environmental technology solutions. The Energy Technology Development and Demonstration Programme supports new technologies in the field of energy that contribute to Denmark's climate objectives. DKK 543 million was made available in the most recent round of funding in 2021. The Ministry of Food, Agriculture and Fisheries runs the Green Development and Demonstration Program, which funds projects that solve important challenges for the Danish food industry while contributing to food, business and environmental policy objectives. In 2020, the programme had a total budget of DKK 259 million.

Funding opportunities are also available to Danish start-ups and scale-ups through the European Innovation Council (EIC), which was established under the EU Horizon Europe programme. The EIC's work programme comprises three programmes: the EIC Accelerator programme, which provides finance to prospective entrepreneurs, start-ups, SMEs and, in rare cases, larger businesses with up to 499 employees, the EIC Accelerator programme, which offers grants for innovation activities as well direct equity investments and convertible loans to support market deployment and scaling up activities, and the EIC Pathfinder programme, which distributes grants of up to EUR 4 million per consortia comprising at least three independent entities established in at least three different eligible countries. The purpose of these grants is to help the selected consortia to develop proofs of concept. Each of these programmes specifically target green entrepreneurship related themes as part of their scope. For instance, the EIC Pathfinder programme will issue challenge calls on the topics of carbon dioxide management and energy storage, while the EIC Transition programme allocates funding for green digital devices and clean energy technologies. Meanwhile, a significant portion of the EUR 1.2 billion allocated to the EIC Accelerator programme in 2022 will be directed to technologies that contribute to meeting the EU's 2030 climate target.

Networks

The Danish Board of Business Development has identified 13 sector strongholds and emerging industries, characterised by their significant contribution to the Danish economy and high level of international competitiveness. Two of these sector strongholds – environmental technology and energy technology – relate closely to the area of green entrepreneurship. In order to strengthen innovation and co-operation within the sector strongholds, a number of cluster organisations were launched in January 2021, with one cluster for each of the sector strongholds. The public funding allocated to the national cluster organisations between 2021 and 2024 is approximately DKK 640 million. In addition, most cluster organisations also receive funding from various national initiatives and European Union (EU) funded programmes.

The national cluster organisations aim to build a bridge between Denmark's research and business communities, hosting events which bring companies, research institutions and policy makers together in order to facilitate the formation of strategic partnerships. The national clusters also support entrepreneurs in realising their growth aspirations by connecting businesses with potential domestic and overseas partners to spur innovation. For instance, the national cluster organisation for the environmental technology sector stronghold (CLEAN) is a partner of the EU Techbridge project, which matches North American customers with European SMEs with innovative water and energy solutions.

Business support services

Denmark's six regional business hubs provide specialised advice to Danish companies, including entrepreneurs, as well as grants and support services to targeted groups. The business hubs serve as a juncture in the business promotion system, helping companies to navigate the various support measures that are available from a range of sources. In 2021, 4 790 businesses received specialised guidance through the business hubs, with three-quarters of these companies also referred to appropriate public or private advisers. Each hub covers multiple municipalities. More localised business development and government administrative services are provided by the municipal business development offices.

The 2022 Agreement on Strong and Innovative Companies also sets aside DKK 1 billion for the formation of eight local business lighthouses, tasked with future-proofing Danish strengths. The majority of these lighthouses will focus on green technology areas. For instance, the business lighthouse for Bornholm will seek to make the island the Baltic Sea's hub for green transport and a centre for offshore wind and green energy testing. Meanwhile, the business lighthouse for North Jutland will promote the region's status as an international leader in the capture, use and storage of CO_2.

In 2019, the Danish Business Authority established the *Virksomhedsguiden* portal. The portal provides entrepreneurs with 24/7 access to information and guidance on the rules and available business support services in Denmark. The website received 1.1 million visits in 2021.

Incubators and accelerators

Denmark has a number of publicly supported business incubators and accelerators, which provide accommodation, guidance, training, contacts and funding to Danish entrepreneurs. These programmes help to nurture early stage start-ups and accelerate the growth of more established businesses. Incubator programmes that are of particular relevance to green entrepreneurs are Beyond Beta's Energy Incubator and the GreenUp Accelerator. Beyond Beta's Energy Incubator, which is partially funded by the EU's Recovery Assistance for Cohesion and the Territories of Europe (REACT-EU) package, provides start-ups with access to entrepreneurial networks, mentoring and workshops, to support in the development of a strategic roadmap for the businesses' development. The GreenUp Accelerator is operated by the Technical University of Denmark's Science Park. It is a 20-month acceleration programme that provides participants with a DKK 1 million convertible loan and more than 75 hours of free counselling, with the ambition of creating climate tech start-ups that are ready to tap into international capital markets.

Exporting support

Support to start-ups and firms looking to export is primarily delivered by EKF. It operates an accelerator programme dedicated to Danish companies looking to export clean technologies. A total of DKK 30 million has been made available to finance preparatory business activities as well as short-term visits to potential export markets. EKF also issues credit guarantees, which allow Danish businesses to offer finance to their overseas customers without assuming any credit risk or delay in payment.

In addition, the exporting capabilities of Danish firms are also supported by the Trade Council of the Ministry of Foreign Affairs. The council has a presence in over 70 countries, and provides businesses with knowledge of local markets and contacts in overseas companies and trade organisations. It also has teams of expert advisors with a specialisation in a number of areas that are of relevance to green entrepreneurs, including energy, water and the environment, and food and agriculture. Through its Incubator Scheme, the Trade Council offers physical and virtual incubation services at 23 locations in 15 countries. Furthermore, the Export Sparring programme supports Danish SMEs in developing an export plan, while the Strategic Business Alliance programme facilitates the exchange of local market knowledge, expertise, networks and resources by bringing together Danish exporters.

Entrepreneurship education

The Danish Foundation for Entrepreneurship runs entrepreneurship programmes for pupils, students and teachers and allocates funds to entrepreneurship projects in educational institutions. The foundation's 2020-25 strategy sets out an aim for 300 000 pupils and students to receive entrepreneurship education during the 2023-24 school year. Another objective is for 20 000 teachers and educators to receive training from the foundation during the strategy period. In order to encourage young people to pursue their entrepreneurial ideas, the foundation also provides grants of up to DKK 50 000 to new enterprises established by students.

Building demand for green entrepreneurs' products and solutions

There is an array of laws, regulations and policy initiatives in place in Denmark that stoke demand for the green goods and services being developed by green entrepreneurs, often by attaching costs to or imposing limits on environmentally unsustainable practices. Many of these measures are at the EU-level.

EU-level measures

Emissions Trading System

The European Union Emissions Trading System (EU ETS) sets a cap on the amount of greenhouse gas emissions that can be emitted by entities covered by the system (European Commission, 2022[13]). This creates a carbon market, whereby emissions allowances are bought, received or traded. This in turn applies a cost to generating greenhouse gas emissions. Currently, the sectors covered by the EU ETS are electricity and heat generation, energy-intensive industrial sectors and commercial aviation within the European Economic Area. However, the European Commission has published proposals to expand the coverage of the EU ETS to include maritime activities and to introduce a separate emissions trading system for fuels used in road transport and buildings. Alongside this, the European Commission is proposing to establish a related Social Climate Fund, whose size will be linked to revenues from the auctioning of emissions allowances under the emissions trading system for fuels. This fund would finance measures and investments to increase energy efficiency, decarbonise the heating and cooling of buildings, and improve access to zero and low emission-emission transport.

Effort Sharing Regulation

The EU's Effort Sharing legislation establishes binding targets for EU Member States to reduce their greenhouse gas emissions from sectors not covered by the EU ETS. The targets set differ across countries. The target for Denmark is to reduce greenhouse gas emissions by 39% relative to 2005 levels, which is the joint-third highest targeted reduction in the EU. While the sectors covered by the EU ETS are regulated at the EU-level, Member States are responsible for implementing policies relating to sectors covered by the Effort Sharing Regulation.

Land use, forestry and agriculture regulations

EU legislation requires Member States to ensure that greenhouse gas emissions arising from land use are fully balanced by an equivalent removal of CO_2 from the atmosphere (European Parliament, 2018[14]). This incentivises more climate-friendly land use and practices.[2] The European Commission has also published proposals for changes to the regulatory framework in this area, with the objective of reaching climate neutrality in the EU's combined land use, forestry and agriculture sector by 2035. The proposals include setting explicit CO_2 removal targets for each Member State.

Danish measures

Climate targets

The 2020 Climate Act establishes the target of reducing Denmark's greenhouse gas emissions in 2030 by 70% compared to the 1990 level. The law also stipulates that at least every five years, a new national climate target must be set for the subsequent ten-year period that is at least as ambitious as its predecessor. Furthermore, the Danish Council on Climate Change reports annually to the Minister for Climate, Energy and Utilities on Denmark's progress in relation to its climate targets. This framework helps to ensure that the green transition remains a continued area of focus for policy makers. The policy stability that this provides can also encourage individuals and businesses to invest in green technologies, products and solutions.

Greening of energy and industry

The Climate Agreement for Energy and Industry 2020 includes a number of measures that will bolster the demand for green goods and services in Denmark. These include tax incentives to accelerate the transition of the heating sector away from fossil fuels and towards green district heating or electric heat pumps, energy savings requirements for public buildings, and investments in renewable energy and green tech.

Waste management

The Climate Agreement for Waste Management sets out a commitment to create a climate-neutral waste sector by 2030 by transitioning from incineration to recycling. This agreement includes measures to improve recycling companies' access to recyclable waste and support businesses in developing and implementing technologies for recycling.

The Danish Government's Action Plan for Circular Economy sets out a variety of steps that can help to prevent and manage waste. These include the mandatory use of eco-labels in public procurement, the provision of guidance and professional advice, extended producer responsibility for packaging, requirements for public tenders, and regulatory changes, including a ban on certain types of single-use plastics. Denmark also has a number of programmes to support businesses in implementing circular economy practices, such as the Green and Circular Transformation in SMEs project in Zealand. These measures stoke demand for the products and solutions being developed by green entrepreneurs.

Public procurement

The Partnership for Green Public Procurement aims to leverage the considerable purchasing power of the public sector in order to support the greening of the Danish economy. Members of the partnership are obliged to follow the partnership's procurement goals and have a publicly available procurement policy which demonstrates that environmental considerations are an essential factor in determining purchasing decisions. Among the members of the partnership are 14 of Denmark's 98 municipalities (including the four most populous municipalities of Copenhagen, Aarhus, Aalborg and Odense), the central and southern regions of Denmark, and the Ministry of the Environment and Food. In 2020, the Ministry of Finance also launched a strategy for green public procurement, which sets out a variety of measures including the purchase of organic foods and eco-labelled products and a commitment to making the public sector vehicle fleet emissions free by 2030.

Policy proposals: building a green entrepreneurship hub

A range of policy recommendations have been developed for the promotion of green entrepreneurship in Denmark. These policy proposals have been developed through a comparative analysis with policy actions in Canada, Germany and Israel, which seeks to identify practices that could be used to address policy gaps in Denmark (see Chapter 4 for the country case studies and a discussion of the lessons learned). Table 1.1 provides a summary of these proposals, along with the entities that should be responsible for overseeing the implementation of each of the recommendations.

Table 1.1. Summary of policy recommendations and responsible entities

Policy recommendation	Responsible entities
1. Develop a unified green entrepreneurship strategy with periodic monitoring reports	• Ministry of Industry, Business and Financial Affairs • Ministry of Climate, Energy and Utilities • Ministry of Environment and Food • Statistics Denmark
2. Develop a one-stop shop for green entrepreneurship support	• Danish Business Authority • Relevant government ministries
3. Support specialised incubators and accelerators that build on local advantages	• Danish Board of Business Development • Danish Business Authority, as a secretariat of the Danish Board of Business Development • Ministry of Higher Education and Science • Selected universities

4. Co-ordinate with private sector actors in the design and implementation of programmes	• Selected private incubators and accelerators • Danish Board of Business Development • Danish Business Authority, as a secretariat of the Danish Board of Business Development • Innovation Fund Denmark
5. Help green entrepreneurs to access global markets	• EKF • Trade Council of the Ministry of Foreign Affairs of Denmark • Innovation Centre Denmark • CLEAN • Energy Cluster Denmark
6. Unleash the potential of public procurement as a driver of change	• Ministry of Finance • Government ministries responsible for purchasing decisions • National Centre for Public Sector Innovation (CO-PI) • Partnership for Green Public Procurement
7. Seek to ensure that regulatory frameworks are conducive to green entrepreneurship	• Danish Business Authority • Relevant government ministries
8. Harness consumers' environmental concerns to stoke demand for green products	• Danish Business Authority • Ecolabelling Denmark • Danish Environmental Protection Agency • Danish Veterinary and Food Administration • Danish Competition and Consumer Authority
9. Expand green entrepreneurship training and education	• Ministry of Higher Education and Science • Ministry of Children and Education • Selected educational and research institutions, including universities, vocational institutes and GTS Institutes.
10. Foster the development of networks within the green entrepreneurship ecosystem	• Relevant national cluster organisations, including CLEAN and Energy Cluster Denmark • Private cluster organisations
11. Tailor support programmes to reflect the needs of green entrepreneurs in different sectors and at different stages of development	• Danish Export and Investment Fund • Innovation Fund Denmark • Danish Board of Business Development

1. Develop a unified green entrepreneurship strategy with periodic monitoring reports

Denmark's green entrepreneurship ecosystem could be strengthened by mapping the various policy actors operating within the ecosystem and then developing a unified green entrepreneurship strategy. Denmark has a number of public policy initiatives in place that can foster green entrepreneurship, ranging from the provision of finance through the Danish Growth Fund, Innovation Fund Denmark and the Danish Green Investment Fund to the support of national cluster organisations that specialise in environmental fields. However, the public organisations that support green entrepreneurs often operate independently with a distinct set of priorities and objectives and there is a low level of awareness about the roles of the various actors involved in supporting green entrepreneurship. The development of the unified strategy would help to facilitate the co-ordination of public efforts to build a green entrepreneurship hub in Denmark and ensure that different organisations are pulling in the same direction. The Pan-Canadian Framework on Clean Growth and Climate Change (PCF) could be a model for developing a unified green entrepreneurship strategy (see Chapter 4).

The development of a unified strategy could be led by a dedicated leadership team or task force, with representatives from relevant public authorities, the Danish Export and Investment Fund, Innovation Fund Denmark, selected national cluster organisations, the regional business hubs and prominent universities. This team would have the remit of monitoring progress, bringing together public actors and recommending changes where appropriate.

The unified strategy should contain a set of shared strategic objectives, key performance indicators (KPIs), targets and policy actions which inform the activities of relevant public actors, taking into account the various recommendations and measures described in this report. The KPIs could be a mix of indicators that relate directly to green entrepreneurship (e.g. number of green start-ups, scale-ups or gazelles, and the corresponding number of jobs, turnover and exports) and indicators that relate to broader sustainability outcomes. More indirect metrics, such as the contribution of the green economy to GDP or employment or levels of funding leveraged, may also be appropriate. The scope of green entrepreneurship encompasses multiple sectors, groups and technologies, which should be taken into account when identifying relevant stakeholders, priorities and actions.

To monitor the implementation of the strategy, the task force could oversee the development of periodic reports on the state of green entrepreneurship in Denmark, which would provide an update on the initiatives that are in place and the progress that has been made towards green entrepreneurship targets. These regular reports could also provide a basis for revising and updating the strategy for fostering green entrepreneurship in Denmark in a way that is responsive to policy experiences, market trends and climate developments. It is important to note that, while having a dynamic approach can be beneficial given the fast changing nature of the green entrepreneurship field, this should be balanced with the need to provide participants in the green entrepreneurship ecosystem with stability and clarity over the future course of public policies, initiatives and incentives.

Data is key to monitoring the implementation of the unified green entrepreneurship strategy, as well as to assessing the overall health of the green entrepreneurship ecosystem and Denmark's progress in the green transition. To facilitate this, it would be instructive to create a green entrepreneurship data strategy, drawing inspiration from Canada's Clean Technology Data Strategy (see Chapter 4). This strategy should establish a clear and consistent understanding of which businesses are included within the scope of green entrepreneurship, which could be defined in collaboration with Statistics Denmark. It should also include the development of periodic publications that provide timely information on the number of green start-ups and scale-ups in Denmark, the sectors they operate in, and the economic footprint they generate, in terms of employment, revenue and gross value added. The green entrepreneurship data strategy could form part of a broader green economy data strategy, which monitors the steps being taken by established businesses to implement green solutions and reduce their environmental impact. An option here would be to introduce an environmental indicator(s) to the existing Business Tendency Surveys. In order to swiftly identify emerging trends, it could also be beneficial to develop new sources of data, such as recurring surveys of green start-ups, similar to the approach used for the Green Startup Monitor in Germany (see Chapter 4).

To inform future policy directions and ensure that public funds are being used effectively, it is important to assess whether the initiatives laid out in the strategy are having their intended impact on green entrepreneurship outcomes. This can be achieved through the development and implementation of a monitoring and evaluation strategy for green entrepreneurship policy initiatives, which could form part of the unified green entrepreneurship strategy. Where feasible, this should include impact evaluations for specific programmes, which involve comparing outcomes among businesses participating in a programme (the treatment group) with those of comparable businesses that are not participating in the programme (the control group).

2. Develop a one-stop shop for green entrepreneurship support

Denmark's six regional hubs, together with the *Virksomhedsguiden* portal, aim to operate as a one-stop shop for Danish entrepreneurs and SMEs, providing a roadmap for entrepreneurs to navigate the various support options and schemes that are available to them. There is a clear demand for these services, with the portal receiving 1.1 million website visits in 2021. However, there is currently insufficient visibility of green entrepreneurship initiatives in these information hubs. This information gap will grow as the scale and scope of initiatives for green entrepreneurs becomes larger and more complex. The six regional hubs and the *Virksomhedsguiden* portal could give greater visibility about events, organisations, schemes, opportunities and projects that are of relevance to green entrepreneurs.

Given the range of parties involved within green entrepreneurship ecosystems, it is important to provide both virtual and physical single points of contact, where all relevant information can be gathered and provided to green entrepreneurs, start-ups, researchers, and any other interested citizens or entities. It is also important for policy initiatives to distinguish between the two distinct activities of implementing existing green solutions and developing new green solutions. Green entrepreneurs, as defined in this report, are principally engaged in the latter. While the *Virksomhedsguiden* portal does currently have a page for green businesses, the focus is predominantly on the greening of established businesses through the implementation of green technologies. A good starting point would therefore be to create a dedicated page for green entrepreneurs on the *Virksomhedsguiden* portal, which targets entrepreneurs with innovative green solutions looking to bring these ideas to market. Strengthening signposting services can boost the uptake of public programmes. For instance, the value of loans issued through the Danish Green Investment Fund is currently well below the allocated limit, suggesting that increased awareness of the programme among entrepreneurs and other entities could help this scheme to achieve a greater reach and impact.

3. Support specialised incubators and accelerators that build on local advantages

Business incubators and accelerators play an important role in stimulating the emergence and growth of new enterprises yet there are few specialised programmes for green entrepreneurs in Denmark. The specialisation in green activities and technologies allows for the delivery of tailored advice, coaching, facilities and infrastructure. They can also bring together businesses, investors and other relevant stakeholders that support green entrepreneurs, facilitating the formation of networks and strategic partnerships, as well as knowledge spill-overs and resource sharing.

Two different approaches can be used to increase the availability of specialised incubation and acceleration programmes for green entrepreneurs. First, increased financial support could be provided to incubators and accelerators that specialise in green technologies so that they can scale up their activities. Alternatively, a greater number of dedicated programmes for green entrepreneurs could be introduced within existing incubators and accelerators. For example, there is experience and expertise within the Beyond Beta start-up programme in the areas of environmental technologies, energy technologies and the circular economy, through the involvement of the national cluster organisations. These knowledge resources could be leveraged by developing programmes within Beyond Beta that are dedicated to cohorts of green entrepreneurs in Denmark. Inspiration could be drawn from Israel's approach to creating theme-based incubators by selecting and funding private organisations to manage the incubators through a competitive tender process. The Israel Innovation Authority recently announced the formation of five incubators, one of which will focus on nurturing climate tech start-ups (see Chapter 4).

Green incubators and accelerators in Denmark would also benefit from building local assets and sources of comparative advantage into their value proposition. These include supporting new start-ups in offshore wind and energy efficient technologies. Two models of how to nest incubation programmes within a specialised ecosystem were identified in Canada, namely Start-up Yard at the Centre for Ocean Ventures and Entrepreneurship and the MaRS Discovery District (see Chapter 4). The former utilises its proximity to the water in order to attract ocean start-ups, while the latter focuses on the benefits that the density of its urban location can bring in terms of networking, knowledge transfer and relationship building. Both have been effective at building international relationships with a range of actors to support entrepreneurs within the incubators and to attract new entrepreneurs to the programmes.

4. Engage with private sector actors in the design and implementation of programmes

To ensure that resources are directed towards areas that can deliver results for Denmark in the future, both economically and environmentally, the focus of public support measures should be sensitive to cues from the private sector and responsive to fast-moving developments in technologies and markets. In all three case study countries, many of the public initiatives to foster green entrepreneurship are strengthened by collaborations with the private sector. For instance, through its Incubator Programme, the Israel Innovation Authority (IIA) invites private groups to apply to operate an incubator that focuses on a particular area. The IIA then provides the incubators with 85% of the initial budget of investments. The IIA's decisions as to which fields or technologies to support are informed to a large extent by signals from the private sector, in order to ensure that the industries being promoted are competitive and commercially viable.

5. Help green entrepreneurs to access global markets

Denmark has a relatively small domestic market, which means that tapping into overseas markets is particularly important for entrepreneurs in realising their growth ambitions. Data compiled by Statistics Denmark suggest that green start-ups in Denmark are slightly less likely to export than other Danish start-ups – 12% of start-ups in the environmental technology sector were exporters in 2019, compared to 13% of start-ups across all sectors. Policies can support green entrepreneurs in this area by building knowledge of overseas markets and fostering links with international businesses, customers and investors. A number of supports are already in place such as the EKF's Green Accelerator programme, but these could be scaled up to help green entrepreneurs reach overseas markets. Another potentially potent tool is the formation of partnerships between Danish incubators or cluster organisations and their international counterparts, which can provide "soft-landings" for green entrepreneurs as they enter overseas markets. International connections can be created, for instance, by reaching out to universities or incubators with complementary programmes, participating in ecosystem visits and contacting consulates to invite international start-ups to visit Danish incubators or clusters.

6. Unleash the potential of public procurement as a driver of change

Public procurement is an area of great potential, with Danish public sector purchases of goods and services amounting to an estimated EUR 50 billion per year (State of Green, 2020[15]). Through the Partnership for Green Public Procurement, Denmark already has in place a ready-to-go framework for raising the demand for green entrepreneurs' products and solutions. At present, only a minority of municipalities and regions are included in the partnership. Expanding the coverage of the partnership to cover the rest of Denmark would go a long way in helping to create a marketplace that is more conducive to green entrepreneurship. Inspiration can also be drawn from Germany's public procurement regulations, which establish strict criteria for the environmental sustainability of publicly procured goods or services. These include a requirement to, where possible, develop lifecycle forecasts of greenhouse gas emissions caused by procured goods and services.

7. Seek to ensure that regulatory frameworks are conducive to green entrepreneurship

Although regulatory frameworks play a major role in quality assurance and creating a market for green solutions, they can also act as a hurdle for green entrepreneurship. For instance, product market regulations that impose excessive barriers to entry have the potential to restrict competition and stifle entrepreneurship (OECD, 2013[16]). Some of the key sectors that green entrepreneurs operate in, such as energy and water, are susceptible to competition deficits and barriers to entry due to the network effects that are inherent to these industries. It is therefore important to ensure that legal and regulatory frameworks do not become bottlenecks but rather act as catalysts for the development and market penetration of innovative green solutions created by green entrepreneurs. It should be acknowledged, however, that a significant number of regulations are at the EU-level, which limits the ability of domestic policy makers to implement changes.

Denmark could consider the adoption of special measures in order to accelerate the pace at which green entrepreneurship projects can navigate through the regulatory framework. These measures could include support in developing proofs of concept, the provision of pilot sites for testing solutions or the introduction of fast licensing arrangements. In some cases, it may also be appropriate to define free zones for green technologies, where special legal or regulatory environments are applied to nurture the fast development and testing of new and innovative green solutions. Regulatory test zones are already in place in Denmark for selected businesses with innovative solutions in the energy sector. Businesses can apply for a regulatory test zone if a number of criteria are met, including that their project promotes the green transition and its implementation is impeded by regulatory barriers.

8. Harness consumers' environmental concerns to stoke demand for green products

The European Commission's latest Eurobarometer survey shows that Danish citizens are among the most environmentally conscious in Europe. The high level of environmental awareness and concern held by consumers is a significant asset for Denmark in its effort to build a hub for green entrepreneurship. A range of measures can be used to leverage this awareness to influence the behaviour of businesses and their supply chains, creating opportunities for green entrepreneurs.

Eco-labelling can be a powerful tool in helping green entrepreneurs in Denmark to build a strong customer base. According to the 2019 Nordic Consumer Survey, 90% of Nordic consumers recognise the Nordic Swan Ecolabel while half of these actively look out for this label when they shop. Green entrepreneurs could benefit from targeted programmes that boost awareness of the option of eco-labelling, provide information on how to apply and provide financial assistance where needed in order to obtain the certification. Support in this area is already being provided by the six Danish Business Hubs via their subsidy schemes, through which businesses can apply for grants to contribute towards the costs of their eco-labelling applications. In Canada, the Business Development Bank of Canada (BDC) has a similar programme in place to help companies receive B Corp certification (see Chapter 4). Continued progress in expanding the list of product groups eligible for eco-labelling would further strengthen Denmark's green entrepreneurship ecosystem by building the demand for green products. For instance, neither the Nordic Swan Ecolabel or the EU-Ecolabel are currently available for food products, which is an area that could be explored in the future.

Another mechanism for bolstering demand for the products and services developed by green entrepreneurs is through climate-related disclosure requirements. These compel large companies to publish information such as their level of greenhouse gas (GHG) emissions and their approach to managing climate-related risks. In October 2021, the Canadian Securities Administrators published details of a proposed instrument that would oblige publicly listed companies to satisfy a number of climate-related reporting requirements. A 2020 study by KPMG found that 88% of the 2 000 largest Danish companies either opted out of reporting their GHG emissions or did not adopt the World Resources Institute's GHG protocol in their reporting. More stringent reporting requirements for large Danish companies could enhance awareness of environmental impacts and risks among consumers and, in particular, investors and other businesses in the supply chain. This in turn could induce a shift towards greener products and solutions within supply chains, creating new market opportunities for green start-ups.

9. Expand green entrepreneurship training and education

Green entrepreneurship education and training can help build a pipeline of green entrepreneurs by stimulating interest among students and helping them develop their capabilities. This is particularly the case in Denmark, where high levels of public engagement on environmental issues create a strong opportunity to provide green entrepreneurship education and training by intersecting entrepreneurship topics with sustainability challenges, concerns or applications. Danish universities are increasingly examining their activities in relation to wider environmental policies or objectives, which is affecting the structure and content of the learning they provide. Some already have agendas in place that to ensure that their operations are consistent with environmental goals. Green entrepreneurship teaching activities can be a strong component of such agendas.

Denmark already has a considerable number of public entities that contribute to green entrepreneurship awareness, teaching and learning. These include the Danish Foundation for Entrepreneurship, the *Virksomhedsguiden* portal, the Danish Business Hubs, the municipality development offices and the Trade Council of the Ministry of Foreign Affairs. By forming partnerships with these public entities and other elements of the green entrepreneurship ecosystem, Denmark's excellent higher education institutions can further improve their offering of sustainability education and green entrepreneurship programmes to a variety of target audiences.

10. Foster the development of networks within the green entrepreneurship ecosystem

Entrepreneurship networks comprised of entrepreneurs, established businesses, research institutions, support organisations, investors, and other private, non-profit and public actors can help start-ups and early-stage businesses overcome skills gaps and improve access to resources. Denmark has invested in building formal networks through the creation of 14 national cluster organisations in the sector strongholds and emerging industries identified by the Business Promotion in Denmark 2020-23 strategy. Membership levels of the national cluster organisations are relatively low, ranging from approximately 200 in the Danish environmental cluster (CLEAN) to more than 500 in the digital technologies cluster. According to data provided by Statistics Denmark, there were more than 9 000 Danish companies in the environmental technology sector in 2019, suggesting that further progress can be made in growing the networks surrounding the national cluster organisations.

The impact of the cluster organisations can be lifted through measures to raise awareness and visibility of the benefits that membership can bring to start-ups, for example through informational campaigns or the dissemination of information via the regional business hubs or the *Virksomhedsguiden* portal. In addition, cluster organisations could engage more start-ups by offering targeted incentives. This could include, for example, exemptions from membership fees, which is not currently the case with all of the cluster organisations. In addition, cluster organisations could be made more relevant for start-ups by increasing their representation in the leadership and/or board membership.

11. Tailor support programmes to reflect the needs of green entrepreneurs in different sectors and at different stages of development

Rather than adopting a one-size-fits-all approach, green entrepreneurship policies and initiatives should be tailored to reflect the different needs of green start-ups and early-stage businesses that operate in different sectors and technology areas. Where appropriate, separate sets of public policies, initiatives and incentives should be implemented for low-tech and high-tech green entrepreneurial ventures. Low-tech green entrepreneurship projects, which could include, for example, a plant-based restaurant or a consultancy firm that advises businesses or consumers on energy efficiency, have different policy needs to high-tech green entrepreneurship projects, such as the development of renewable energy. Even within the category of high-tech green entrepreneurs, the most appropriate policy measures will depend on the corresponding technology readiness levels and will change according to the maturity of the projects.

Green entrepreneurship support offers in Denmark currently favour high-tech start-ups but more can be done to tailor the initiatives offered by entities such as the Danish Growth Fund, Innovation Fund Denmark and Danish Green Investment Fund to the needs of entrepreneurs working on different technologies and at different stages of development. The BDC in Canada is a good case study of co-ordinating and articulating policy support in this way, bringing also a whole of government approach that actively includes several segments of the population in an inclusive way (see Chapter 4). Moreover, even if cleantech is one of the main policy priorities, it is important that low-tech projects also receive public visibility and support because they also have a role in contributing to the achievement of overall environmental and entrepreneurship policy goals. The case study countries offer some examples of initiatives that support low-tech green entrepreneurs, including the SwitchMed project in Israel that supports green entrepreneurs with non-tech start-ups and the DBU's Green Startup Programme in Germany (see Chapter 4).

References

Escalona, C. (2021), *Mapping the Danish Cleantech Startup ecosystem: Understanding the economic potential of the Cleantech sector and challenges facing new Cleantech ventures*, TechBBQ. [10]

European Commission (2022), *EU Emissions Trading System (EU ETS)*, https://ec.europa.eu/clima/eu-action/eu-emissions-trading-system-eu-ets_en (accessed on 31 May 2022). [13]

European Commission (2021), *Eurobarometer: Optimism about the future of the EU at its highest since 2009*, https://europa.eu/eurobarometer/surveys/detail/2532 (accessed on 24 February 2022). [1]

European Parliament (2018), "Regulation (EU) 2018/841 of the European Parliament and of the Council of 30 May 2018 on the inclusion of greenhouse gas emissions and removals from land use, land use change and forestry in the 2030 climate and energy framework, and amending Regulation (EU) No 525/2013 and Decision No 529/2013/EU", *Official Journal of the European Union*. [14]

Eurostat (2022), *GDP and main components (output, expenditure and income)*, https://appsso.eurostat.ec.europa.eu/nui/show.do?dataset=nama_10_gdp&lang=en (accessed on 24 February 2022). [7]

International Energy Agency (2022), *Data and statistics*, https://www.iea.org/data-and-statistics/data-browser?country=WORLD&fuel=CO2%20emissions&indicator=TotCO2 (accessed on 24 February 2022). [6]

IRIS Group & CLEAN (2019), *Analyse af energiteknologiklyngen*, https://www.energycluster.dk/wp-content/uploads/2021/02/1066682245.pdf (accessed on 24 February 2022). [3]

Ministry of Industry, B. (2021), *Statement about Green Business Adjustment*. [9]

OECD (2022), *Environmental tax*, https://data.oecd.org/envpolicy/environmental-tax.htm (accessed on 24 February 2022). [8]

OECD (2022), *OECD Patent Statistics*, https://www.oecd-ilibrary.org/science-and-technology/data/oecd-patent-statistics_patent-data-en (accessed on 24 February 2022). [2]

OECD (2022), *Patents on environment technologies* (indicator), https://doi.org/10.1787/fff120f8-en (accessed on 24 February 2022). [5]

OECD (2021), *Building the STRING megaregion as a green hub in the wake of COVID-19*, OECD, Paris. [4]

OECD (2013), *Working Party on SMEs and Entrepreneurship (WPSMEE) - Green entrepreneurship, Eco-innovation and SMEs*, OECD. [16]

Startup Genome (2022), *The Global Startup Ecosystem Report Cleantech Edition*. [11]

State of Green (2020), *Green purchasing for a green future: The Danish government flexes the public procurement muscle*, https://stateofgreen.com/en/partners/state-of-green/news/green-purchasing-for-a-green-future-the-danish-government-flexes-the-public-procurement-muscle/ (accessed on 25 February 2022). [15]

TECH BBQ (2022), *TECH BBQ Impact Series*, https://www.techbbq.blog/impact-series (accessed on 24 February 2022). [12]

Notes

[1] The 2020 figures for GDP and CO2 emissions will have been distorted by the effects of the COVID-19 pandemic.

[2] Biomass and soils act as a sink for CO_2. The use of land or changes in the use of land can therefore have an effect on the amounts of CO_2 in the atmosphere, by triggering CO_2 flows between terrestrial CO_2 reservoirs and the atmosphere.

2 The importance of green entrepreneurship

The Danish Council on Climate Change estimated that only one-third of Denmark's targeted reductions in greenhouse gas emissions by 2030 can be achieved through existing policy measures. This means that technological innovation is critical if Denmark is to achieve its climate objectives. Green entrepreneurs can have a key role to play both in developing these innovations and in bringing them to market. This chapter provides an introduction to the need for and drivers of green entrepreneurship. It also develops the definition of green entrepreneurship that is adopted throughout this report.

Highlights

- The United Nation's (UN) Intergovernmental Panel on Climate Change's (IPCC) most recent report has re-affirmed that human activities have fuelled changes in climate that are "unprecedented in thousands, if not hundreds of thousands of years". This is already having a devastating global impact through an increased prevalence of natural disasters and extreme weather events.
- Combatting climate change is of critical importance to maintaining wellbeing and standards of living across the world. In order to avoid the most severe economic, social and environmental consequences, climate experts warn that the temperature rise must be limited to 1.5°C. The IPCC assesses that this will necessitate rapid and large-scale reductions in greenhouse gas (GHG) emissions.
- Entrepreneurs can be a significant driving force behind efforts to lower GHG emissions through their capacity to develop and propagate innovative green solutions. Public policies that promote green entrepreneurship can therefore play a decisive role in the global effort to mitigate human-induced climate change.
- Definitions and terminologies used to describe the notion of green entrepreneurship vary widely across different countries and studies. This report adopts the following definition of green entrepreneurship:
    - Green entrepreneurship encompasses the development and deployment by new start-ups of green products, services and processes, i.e. those that either:
        - reduce or prevent any type of environmental damage; or
        - emit less pollution and waste, or are more resource-efficient than equivalent normal products, services and process that have the same result. Their primary use, however, is not one of environmental protection.
- There is an array of factors that influence and drive green entrepreneurship. These include the policy landscape, economic conditions, societal attitudes, technological developments, legal and regulatory frameworks, and environmental pressures.

The need for green entrepreneurship

Entrepreneurs have an important role in bringing new ideas to the market and driving change in economies. This is particularly true for green entrepreneurship, where new start-ups have the potential to disrupt established practices (Phan, Siegel and Wright, 2005[1]). However, entrepreneurship always entails risk and it is estimated that only 1-2% of inventions reach the market (Braunerhjelm et al., 2009[2]). Technology innovation – including climate technology – is subject to even greater levels of risk due to higher uncertainty (e.g. unclear market demand, regulatory uncertainty). This is further complicated for climate technologies because social returns typically exceed private returns (Gompers and Lerner, 2001[3]). Thus, the promotion of green entrepreneurship is complex. There are high fixed costs in the research and development stages and high risks in the commercialisation phase, suggesting that a reliance on private markets alone without government intervention would be suboptimal (Popp, 2012[4]).

The United Nation's (UN) Intergovernmental Panel on Climate Change's (IPCC) most recent report has re-affirmed that human activities have fuelled changes in climate that are "unprecedented in thousands, if not hundreds of thousands of years" (Intergovernmental Panel on Climate Change, 2021[5]), with the UN Secretary General describing the report as a "code red for humanity". Global average temperatures are approximately 1.1 degrees Celsius (°C) above 1850-1900 levels, with this change attributable to greenhouse gas (GHG) emissions associated with human activities (Intergovernmental Panel on Climate Change, 2021[5]).

Climate change is already having devastating impacts on societies across the world, including an increased incidence of wildfires (Abatzoglou and Williams, 2016[6]) (Jan Van Oldenborgh et al., 2021[7]) and droughts (Dai, 2011[8]). With global temperatures increasing at a rate of nearly 0.2°C per decade (Lindsey and Dahlman, 2021[9]), these impacts are set to become significantly more severe over the coming decades (Dellink, Lanzi and Chateau, 2019[10]) (Intergovernmental Panel on Climate Change, 2021[5]). In order to avoid the most severe economic, social and environmental consequences, climate experts warn that the temperature rise should be limited to 1.5°C (IPCC, 2018[11]). However, the IPCC's Sixth Assessment Report finds that "unless there are immediate, rapid and large-scale reductions in greenhouse gas emissions, limiting warming to close to 1.5°C or even 2°C will be beyond reach" (Figure 2.1) (Intergovernmental Panel on Climate Change, 2021[5]).

Figure 2.1. Global warming by 2100 depends on climate policies

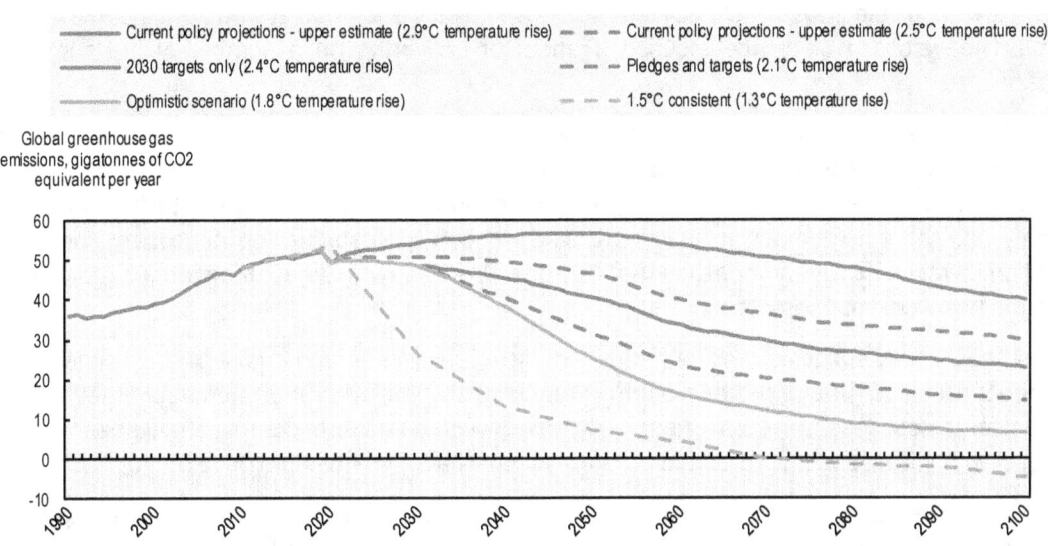

Source: (Climate Action Tracker, 2021[12])

StatLink https://stat.link/n84zd9

Reducing greenhouse gas emissions is the principle way in which the world's environmental crises can be mitigated. Some initial progress has been made on this front, with GHG emissions from OECD countries having fallen since 2007 as a result of a strengthening of climate policies and the economic slowdown associated with the global financial crisis in 2008 (OECD, 2020[13]). In the medium- to long-term, economic growth and reductions in GHG emissions are complementary rather than conflicting objectives. Indeed, it is estimated that the GDP of G20 countries would be 4.7% higher in 2050 in a scenario where policy interventions ensure that climate damage is avoided relative to a scenario where no actions are taken (OECD, 2017[14]).

Entrepreneurs can be a significant driving force behind efforts to lower GHG emissions through their capacity to develop and propagate innovative green solutions. Green entrepreneurship is therefore an emerging field of interest in a world confronted with the need to achieve economic growth while making frugal use of natural resources and minimising pollution (Potluri and Phani, 2020[15]). Public policies that promote green entrepreneurship can play a decisive role in the global effort to mitigate human-induced climate change.

Defining green entrepreneurship

A number of broader concepts such as green growth and sustainable development need to be clarified before turning to green entrepreneurship. The OECD Green Growth Strategy notes that green growth implies fostering economic growth and development, while ensuring that natural assets continue to provide the resources and environmental services on which our well-being relies (Box 2.1). This is more narrow than sustainable development, which considers a wider range of social factors as outlined in the UN's Sustainable Development Goals (SDGs).

Box 2.1. Green growth and sustainable development

Sustainable development provides an important context for green growth. The OECD Green Growth Strategy leverages the substantial body of analysis and policy effort that flowed from the 1992 Rio Earth Summit. It develops a clear and focused agenda for delivering on a number of the summit's key aspirations.

Green growth has not been conceived as a replacement for sustainable development. It should instead be considered as a subset of sustainable development. It is narrower in scope, entailing an operational policy agenda that can help achieve concrete, measurable progress at the interface between the economy and the environment. It provides a strong focus on fostering the necessary conditions for innovation, investment and competition that can give rise to new sources of economic growth that are consistent with resilient ecosystems.

Policies need to pay specific attention to many of the social issues and equity concerns that can arise as a direct result of greening the economy – both at the national and international levels. This is essential for the successful implementation of green growth policies. Measures should be implemented in parallel with initiatives centred on the broader social pillar of sustainable development.

The OECD Green Growth Strategy develops an actionable policy framework that is designed to be flexible enough to be tailored to differing national circumstances and stages of development. In partnership with initiatives by other international organisations, including UNEP, UNESCAP and the World Bank, the OECD's work on green growth has been planned to contribute to the objectives of the 2012 UN Conference on Sustainable Development (Rio+20).

Source: (OECD, 2011[16])

Entrepreneurship has an important role to play in making progress towards green growth objectives. In general, entrepreneurship is widely recognised as boosting economic activity and stimulating job creation (OECD, 2020[17]). Increasingly, entrepreneurship is also being recognised as a means of addressing societal challenges, including environmental sustainability. The role of entrepreneurs in this area is twofold:

1. By developing and bringing to market innovative products, entrepreneurs can propagate environmentally sustainable solutions throughout the economy;
2. By taking steps to improve the environmental sustainability of their businesses, entrepreneurs can collectively have an impact on progress towards green objectives.

Despite much discourse over the past 20 years, a consensus on the definition of green entrepreneurship has yet to emerge. A range of definitions have been proposed for green entrepreneurship and related terms in the academic literature and other research (Table 2.1) and there have been many calls to move towards a consensus (Demirel et al., 2017[18]).

Table 2.1. Defining green entrepreneurship

Definition	Source
"Both Entrepreneurship and Environmentalism are based on a perception of value. The attitudes which inform environmental concerns create areas of value that can be exploited entrepreneurially. 'Environmental Entrepreneurs' not only recognise opportunities, but also construct real organisations to capture and promote changes in society."	(Anderson, 1998[19])
"An ecopreneur is a person who seeks to transform a sector of the economy towards sustainability by starting business in that sector with a green design, with green processes and with the life-long commitment to sustainability in everything that is said and done."	(Isaak, 2002[20])
"We distinguish between two types ecopreneurs… 'environment-conscious entrepreneurs' are well aware of environmental issues, but they are not in the environmental marketplace… The second category of ecopreneurs, called 'green entrepreneurs', are those who are both aware of environmental issues and whose business venture is in the environmental marketplace."	(Thierry Volery, 2002[21])
There are four types of green entrepreneurs: • Ad-hoc enviropreneurs, who are "accidental green entrepreneurs" primarily motivated by financial concerns; • Ethical mavericks who are driven by sustainability considerations and influenced primarily by friends, networks and experience; • Innovative opportunists who are financially oriented and have identified a green opportunity, and; • Visionary champions, who set out "to change the world" and are "active in the transformation of society.	(Walley and Taylor, 2002[22])
"Green community entrepreneurship is…the collective ability to mobilise resources, including social capital, to provide products or services that achieve environmental rather than profit maximising goals."	(Gliedt and Parker, 2007[23])
"Green entrepreneurs exploit the opportunities that are inherent in environmentally relevant market failures; however, the paradox of green entrepreneurship may also emanate from the fact that environmental wellbeing that results from born greens is a public good and, therefore, non-excludable. This property of non-excludability may push green entrepreneurs (along with their nascent breakthrough innovations) into liminal spaces, where additional costs render green entrepreneurs at a competitive disadvantage and, thus, limit their economic impact vis-à-vis non-green actors."	(Demirel et al., 2017[18])
Green entrepreneurs can be mapped to four broad types along 2 dimensions: i) Profit-seeking vs. Social mission; ii) Start-ups vs. Established firms. Each type of green entrepreneurs has different incentives and desired outcomes.	(Nikolaou, Tasopoulou and Tsagarakis, 2018[24])

While these academic concepts are useful for deepening an understanding of green entrepreneurs, including their motivations and activities, it can be difficult for governments to design policy and implement around these notions. In practice, governments tend to use terms and definitions that are based on activities and/or sectors:

- *Cleantech*: This term is commonly used in Canada to describe the types of products and services typically developed by green entrepreneurs. Statistics Canada defines clean technologies as (Statistics Canada, 2021[25]):
    o Any good or service designed with the primary purpose of contributing to remediating or preventing any type of environmental damage;
    o Any good or service that is less polluting or more resource-efficient than equivalent normal products which furnish a similar utility. Their primary use, however, is not one of environmental protection.
- *Greentech*: In Germany, the government tends to use the more narrow concept of greentech, which covers technologies that provide solutions to preserving the environment and/or meet fundamental human needs in a sustainable way (Federal Ministry for the Environment, 2021[26]). This includes technologies in seven lead markets (environmentally friendly power generation, storage and distribution, energy efficiency, material efficiency, sustainable mobility, waste management and recycling, sustainable water management, and sustainable agriculture and forestry), with each lead market further divided into a series market segments and technology lines.

- *Climate tech*: The Israel Innovation Authority defines climate tech companies as those that develop technologies aimed at climate change mitigation and adaptation (Moise, Klar and Siegmann, 2021[27]). Climate change mitigation refers to reducing emissions from various sectors as well as removing CO_2 from the atmosphere. Climate change adaptation refers to building resilience to climate-related risks in order to minimise the adverse impacts of climate change. Climate tech is more a narrow field than cleantech or greentech, which both cover climate-related issues as well as other environmental issues.

Building on previous OECD work on green entrepreneurship (OECD/Eurostat, 1999[28]; OECD, 2011[16]), and recent concepts used in the case study countries, a definition of green entrepreneurship is proposed for Denmark (Box 2.2). This understanding of green entrepreneurship covers entrepreneurs who create and commercialise products by forming new start-ups that help to tackle environmental challenges, rather than the broader population of entrepreneurs and micro businesses who are taking steps to reduce their businesses' environmental footprint. It also focuses on the role of new enterprises in developing green products, as opposed to green innovations taking place within established companies. The definition is not limited to any specific sectors, issues or drivers, and instead seeks to capture the myriad of ways in which the innovative actions of green entrepreneurs can address sustainability concerns. This concept of green entrepreneurship is broadly consistent with previous frameworks for measuring green entrepreneurship (OECD, 2011[29]) but two important advances are put forward. First, it makes a strong distinction between pre start-up and early-stage entrepreneurship activities and those undertaken by existing firms. Second, it does not limit itself to businesses whose primary or secondary activities are in core environmental sectors. Please see (OECD, 2022[30]) for further discussion on measuring green entrepreneurship and the greening activities of SMEs.

Box 2.2. Green entrepreneurship in the Danish context

Green entrepreneurship encompasses the development and deployment by new start-ups of green products, services and processes i.e. those that either:

- reduce or prevent any type of environmental damage; or
- emit less pollution and waste, or are more resource-efficient than equivalent normal products, services and process that have the same result. Their primary use, however, is not one of environmental protection.

"Normal products, services and processes" refers to products, services and processes that are the current standard for the time and context, and as such will vary over time and in different contexts. This definition is therefore dynamic to ensure that it captures *further* progress in improving environmental sustainability.

Drivers of green entrepreneurship

There are a number of key factors that influence and drive green entrepreneurship. At a basic level, green entrepreneurship stems from the need for societies to address environmental challenges. As environmental pressures become more acute and societies increasingly seek to adopt a more sustainable way of living, the demand for green products and solutions increases. Global markets for climate-friendly businesses and technologies are growing. For example, it is estimated that the Paris Agreement has opened up USD 23 trillion of climate-smart investment opportunities in emerging markets between 2016 and 2030 (IFC, 2016[31]).

Policy makers influence the development of green entrepreneurship by setting taxes, environmental regulations and trade policies, as well as implementing measures to encourage the development of new technologies and products and the related emergence and growth of green start-ups. Policies can provide direct support to green entrepreneurs through, for instance, improved access to funding, skills or networks. Indirect policy support can be provided by strengthening environmental and climate policies, which in turn create new market opportunities for green entrepreneurs to exploit. For example, legislation relating to natural resource consumption, waste disposal, carbon dioxide emissions, energy consumption and environmental protection are examples of initiatives that may contribute towards a shift to more circular and sustainable modes of production and consumption.

The performance of the economy, and in particular the environmental economy, also has a significant impact on green entrepreneurship. In the European Union (EU), the environmental economy is growing faster than the overall economy, demonstrating that EU Member States are taking action to support a more sustainable model of economic growth (Figure 2.2). The contribution of the environmental economy to EU GDP increased from 1.6 % in 2000 to 2.3 % in 2018 (Eurostat, 2022[32]). During the same period, employment in the EU environmental economy increased from 3.1 million full-time equivalents to 4.4 million full-time equivalents. Green entrepreneurship is a key contributor to such job creation results. In most cases, these new jobs in the clean economy have different skill profiles to those that may become obsolete. For instance, in the automotive sector, jobs are shifting in favour of IT specialists, power electronics, recycling and battery technologies (Joint Research Centre, 2018[33]).

Figure 2.2. The environmental economy is growing faster than the overall economy

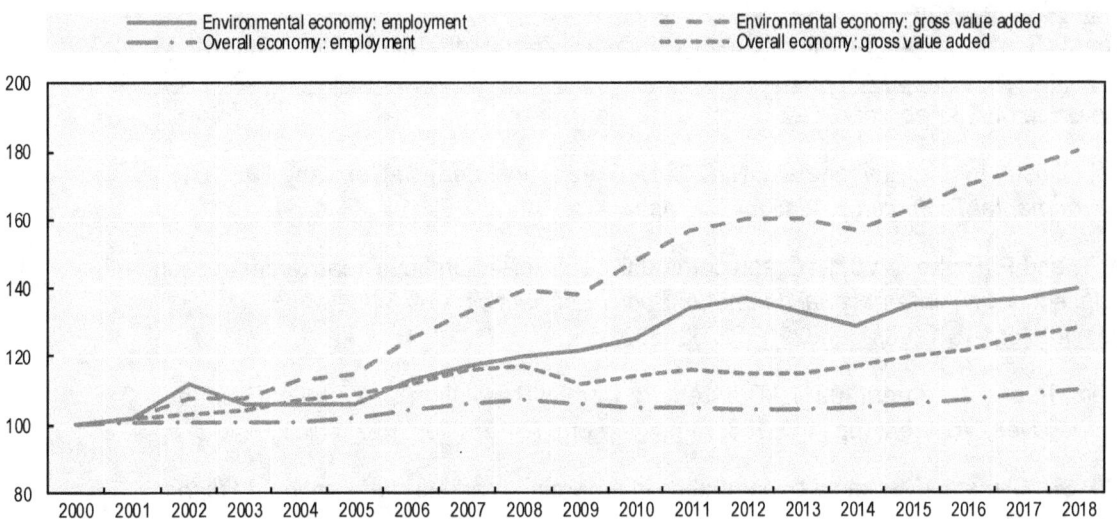

Source: (Eurostat, 2022[32])

StatLink https://stat.link/vjq5ch

References

Abatzoglou, J. and A. Williams (2016), "Impact of anthropogenic climate change on wildfire across western US forests", *Proceedings of the National Academy of Sciences of the United States of America*, Vol. 113/42, https://doi.org/10.1073/pnas.1607171113. [6]

Anderson, A. (1998), *Cultivating the Garden of Eden: Environmental entrepreneuring*, https://doi.org/10.1108/09534819810212124. [19]

Braunerhjelm, P. et al. (2009), "The missing link: knowledge diffusion and entrepreneurship in endogenous growth", *Small Business Economics*, Vol. 34/2, pp. 105-125, https://doi.org/10.1007/s11187-009-9235-1. [2]

Climate Action Tracker (2021), *2100 Warming Projections*, https://climateactiontracker.org/global/temperatures/ (accessed on 24 February 2022). [12]

Dai, A. (2011), *Drought under global warming: A review*, https://doi.org/10.1002/wcc.81. [8]

Dellink, R., E. Lanzi and J. Chateau (2019), "The Sectoral and Regional Economic Consequences of Climate Change to 2060", *Environmental and Resource Economics*, Vol. 72/2, https://doi.org/10.1007/s10640-017-0197-5. [10]

Demirel, P. et al. (2017), "Born to be green: new insights into the economics and management of green entrepreneurship", *Small Business Economics*, Vol. 52/4, pp. 759-771, https://doi.org/10.1007/s11187-017-9933-z. [18]

Eurostat (2022), *Environmental economy – statistics on employment and growth*, https://ec.europa.eu/eurostat/statistics-explained/index.php?title=Environmental_economy_%E2%80%93_statistics_on_employment_and_growth#:~:text=Evolution%20of%20gross%20value%20added%20of%20the%20environmental%20economy,-Gross%20value%20added&text=Gross%20value%20added%20of%20the%20environmental%20economy%20rose%20steadily%20between,in%20all%20years%20after%202014. (accessed on 23 February 2022). [32]

Federal Ministry for the Environment, N. (2021), *GreenTech made in Germany 2021, Environmental Technology Atlas for Germany*. [26]

Gliedt, T. and P. Parker (2007), "Green community entrepreneurship: Creative destruction in the social economy", *International Journal of Social Economics*, Vol. 34/8, https://doi.org/10.1108/03068290710763053. [23]

Gompers, P. and J. Lerner (2001), "The Venture Capital Revolution", *Journal of Economic Perspectives*, Vol. 15/2, pp. 145-168, https://doi.org/10.1257/jep.15.2.145. [3]

IFC (2016), "Climate investment opportunities in emerging markets", *International Finance Comittee*. [31]

Intergovernmental Panel on Climate Change (2021), *Sixth Assessment Report*. [5]

IPCC (2018), *Global warming of 1.5°C*. [11]

Isaak, R. (2002), "The making of the ecopreneur", *Greener Management International* 38, https://doi.org/10.9774/GLEAF.3062.2002.su.00009. [20]

Jan Van Oldenborgh, G. et al. (2021), "Attribution of the Australian bushfire risk to anthropogenic climate change", *Natural Hazards and Earth System Sciences*, Vol. 21/3, https://doi.org/10.5194/nhess-21-941-2021. [7]

Joint Research Centre (2018), *Jobs and skills in the energy transition*. [33]

Lindsey, R. and L. Dahlman (2021), "Climate Change: Global Temperature", *Science & Information for a Climate-Smart Nation*. [9]

Moise, T., U. Klar and A. Siegmann (2021), *Israel's State of Climate Tech 2021*, Israel Innovation Authority & PLANETech. [27]

Nikolaou, I., K. Tasopoulou and K. Tsagarakis (2018), "A Typology of Green Entrepreneurs Based on Institutional and Resource-based Views", *The Journal of Entrepreneurship*, Vol. 27/1, pp. 111-132, https://doi.org/10.1177/0971355717738601. [24]

OECD (2022), "Towards a pilot dashboard of SME greening and green entrepreneurship indicators: Concept note", No. CFE/SME(2022)11. [30]

OECD (2020), *Environment at a Glance 2020*. [13]

OECD (2020), *International Compendium of Entrepreneurship Policies*, OECD Studies on SMEs and Entrepreneurship, OECD Publishing, Paris, https://doi.org/10.1787/338f1873-en. [17]

OECD (2017), *Investing in Climate, Investing in Growth*, OECD Publishing, Paris, https://doi.org/10.1787/9789264273528-en. [14]

OECD (2011), *Entrepreneurship at a Glance 2011*, OECD Publishing, Paris, https://doi.org/10.1787/9789264097711-en. [29]

OECD (2011), *Towards Green Growth*, OECD Green Growth Studies, OECD Publishing, Paris, https://doi.org/10.1787/9789264111318-en. [16]

OECD/Eurostat (1999), *The Environmental Goods and Services Industry: Manual for Data Collection and Analysis*, OECD Publishing, Paris, https://doi.org/10.1787/9789264173651-en. [28]

Phan, P., D. Siegel and M. Wright (2005), "Science parks and incubators: observations, synthesis and future research", *Journal of Business Venturing*, Vol. 20/2, pp. 165-182, https://doi.org/10.1016/j.jbusvent.2003.12.001. [1]

Popp, D. (2012), *The Role of Technological Change in Green Growth*, National Bureau of Economic Research, Cambridge, MA, https://doi.org/10.3386/w18506. [4]

Potluri, S. and B. Phani (2020), "Incentivizing green entrepreneurship: A proposed policy prescription (a study of entrepreneurial insights from an emerging economy perspective)", *Journal of Cleaner Production*, Vol. 259, https://doi.org/10.1016/j.jclepro.2020.120843. [15]

Statistics Canada (2021), *Clean technologies and the Survey of Environmental Goods and Services: A technical reference guide*, https://publications.gc.ca/collections/collection_2021/statcan/16-511-x2021001-eng.pdf (accessed on 24 February 2022). [25]

Thierry Volery (2002), *Ecopreneurship: Rationale, current issues and futures challenges*. [21]

Walley, E. and D. Taylor (2002), "Opportunists, champions, Mavericks . . .? A typology of green entrepreneurs", *Greener Management International* 38, https://doi.org/10.9774/GLEAF.3062.2002.su.00005. [22]

3 International policy trends and practices

Green entrepreneurship is quickly rising up policy agendas across OECD countries, building on the momentum created by the recent COP26 meeting and the opportunities created for green policies through COVID-19 recovery packages. Governments in OECD countries tend to promote and support green entrepreneurship through two main channels, namely direct support packages for entrepreneurs as well as policies and measures that create demand for green products and services. This chapter presents a brief overview of these different potential policy actions and describes how they are implemented in OECD countries.

Highlights

Green entrepreneurship policy

- Governments typically use a combination of different types of policies and schemes to promote and support green entrepreneurship. These include measures that seek to build a demand for green solutions, as well as direct support measures for entrepreneurs.
- Overall, policies and schemes for green entrepreneurship are still in their infancy. Most governments have developed green entrepreneurship supports by adapting instruments used for supporting innovation and entrepreneurship more generally.
- Little is known about the effectiveness of green entrepreneurship support measures but some success factors can be identified from leading international cases, such as building funding pipelines, fostering networks and engaging the private sector.
- Non-government actors can also play an important role in supporting green entrepreneurship. This includes wealthy individual donors who support green projects, as well as cluster and industry organisations that support green innovation and specialised community organisations that offer training or other support services.

Direct support for green entrepreneurs

- One main area of policy intervention is to support the development of green skills among entrepreneurs and help eco-innovators commercialise their work. Some small-scale training programmes have been implemented across OECD countries, but an emerging approach is to provide integrated support packages through dedicated cleantech or climate tech incubator and accelerator programmes. However, there is still only a very small number of such specialised incubator programmes.
- Improving access to finance is another critical area for policy intervention given the greater risks and longer time to market for green innovations. Governments are using a range of debt, equity and hybrid instruments to support green entrepreneurs, often managed through public financial institutions.

Building demand for green solutions

- Governments have made many high-level commitments to move towards a more sustainable economic model. This includes high-level policy frameworks such as the United Nations' Sustainable Development Goals, as well as economic plans such as the European Union's Green Deal. The commitments and plans guide new policy development and help shift social attitudes to create new opportunities for green entrepreneurs. Both of these are critical for creating favourable conditions for green entrepreneurship.
- Another important area of policy work is supporting the development of the circular economy. While there are some examples of national-level policy action, the majority of initiatives (e.g. training, match-making) are driven by local governments.
- Governments are also starting to use green procurement to open up new market opportunities for green entrepreneurs.

Direct supports for green entrepreneurs

Supporting the development of green skills

Entrepreneurs use a wide range of skills in the process of starting and running their business. These include both the workforce skills required of employees (i.e. to "do the job") as well as additional skills that reflect the demands of running a business (e.g. identifying opportunities, financial literacy). Green entrepreneurs often also need an additional set of "green" competences. While there is no generally accepted definition of green skills, they can be considered as the skills needed to adapt products, services and processes to climate change and the related environmental requirements and regulations (OECD/Cedefop, 2014[1]). Some recent data-driven research has gone further in defining different occupational characteristics needed by workers in green jobs. On average, workers in green jobs use more intensively high-level cognitive and interpersonal skills compared to those in non-green jobs. The work content of green jobs is also less routinised, on average, than that of non-green jobs (Consoli et al., 2016[2]).

Governments across the OECD have increased the number of training schemes to support workers in transitioning to green jobs, but "green" entrepreneurship training continues to be quite rare. In addition to training for the circular economy that have been already noted, there have been some short-lived small-scaled schemes in countries such as Canada and Spain. Traditionally green entrepreneurship training schemes have focused on technical skills needed in the trades, often offered in partnership with industry associations, or on green finance. A notable exception is the Green Entrepreneurship Network (*Red Emprendeverde*) in Spain (Fundación Biodiversidad, 2022[3]), which is a platform that was launched by the Biodiversity Foundation (*Fundación Biodiversidad*), a public foundation supported by the National Ministry of Environment and Rural and Marine Development. The network provides support to entrepreneurs and business owners through 1) drafting or redefining business plans; 2) bringing investors and entrepreneurs together; and 3) providing training and technical assistance. It also organises competitions to encourage quality projects while financially supporting some of the most promising initiatives. An increasingly common approach to supporting the development of green skills among entrepreneurs is through dedicated business incubator and accelerator programmes (see next section).

Delivering support packages through green incubators and accelerators

Business incubator and accelerator programmes have been used widely in the United States to support start-ups and early-stage businesses and they are increasingly appearing in other OECD countries. These programmes typically provide a combination of training, individualised coaching and advisory services, access to networks, investors or markets, and traditionally a workspace and shared facilities and equipment. Governments are active in directly offering business incubator and accelerator programmes, and providing financial support to initiatives that are operated by private sector actors.

Estimates from 2017 suggest that there are approximately 2 000 technology incubators and 150 accelerator programmes worldwide, but fewer than 70 specialise in climate technologies (United Nations, 2018[4]). Given the potential benefits of such programmes and high profile success stories such as Climate KIC Europe, it is not clear why so few focus on climate technologies. Two potential factors include the long development time needed for climate technologies, which discourages investors, as well as reluctance among entrepreneurs to be identified as cleantech (Climate-KIC, 2014[5]).

Business incubator and accelerator programmes for climate technologies have both advantages and disadvantages. The main advantage is that incubator programmes are often well-linked to universities and science parks, offering a strong potential to stimulate the commercialisation of new climate innovations and technologies. In addition, there appear to be two recent trends in business incubation that can improve the support offered to start-ups. These are the growing focus by incubators on specific sectors as well as the emphasis on strengthening international networks to help entrepreneurs reach new markets. However, traditional business incubator and accelerator models typically needed to be tailored for start-ups based on high-risk projects such as climate technologies.

Figure 3.1. There are fewer than 100 climate technology incubators worldwide

Number of climate technology incubator and accelerator programmes, 2017

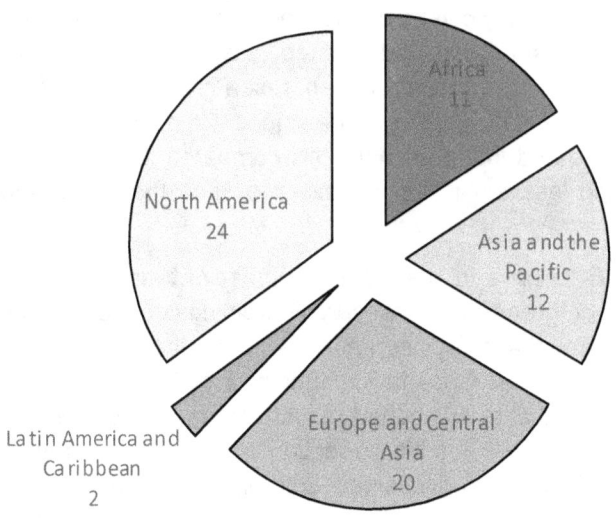

Source: (United Nations, 2018[4])

StatLink https://stat.link/9f7tk6

Facilitating access to green and sustainable finance

Access to finance is a challenge for nearly all entrepreneurs. Green entrepreneurs are often among those who face the greatest obstacles, especially those working in new technologies. Climate technologies have higher uncertainties and costs than other technologies, such as software or medical (United Nations, 2018[4]). These obstacles often stem from a higher risk-return profile since green entrepreneurs' business models (e.g. low carbon innovations) can have long and uncertain development horizons.

A primary barrier faced by green entrepreneurs is the information asymmetry between lender and entrepreneur. In addition, there is often a limited range of sustainable financing products and an insufficient diversity of lenders with appetite for sustainable investments (McDaniels and Robins, 2017[6]). Furthermore, green start-ups typically rely largely on intangible assets, for example intellectual capital. Despite the large contribution that these intangible assets have on their growth and profitability of the firm (OECD, 2018[7]), they are often not recognised by lenders as acceptable collateral in exchange for debt financing. This, in combination with the long time horizon over which green start-ups become profitable, increases the need for more financing options for different stages of the firm's life cycle, and thus is a rationale for policy intervention.

Another challenge faced by green start-ups is that they commonly serve new markets, which can deter lenders and investors given the large uncertainty surrounding potential returns given the unpredictability of future demand. Furthermore, the "niche" nature of green markets can contribute to a limited supply of finance options as: 1) investors and entrepreneurs might share different environmental objectives and ideals; 2) investors and entrepreneurs can have different levels of knowledge about green market; and 3) investors might perceive that green business have additional financial burdens, in addition to greater uncertainty and longer time horizons (OECD, 2013[8]). Indeed, there can be a large incompatibility between investor expectations regarding time horizons and the time green businesses take to develop and enter the market. For example, eco-innovations require a period of 5 to 10 years from product development to market breakthrough, while venture capital firms normally aim to exit from investment in 2 to 3 years (OECD, 2013[8]).

These challenges have led governments, lenders and investors to respond with new financial products, commonly referred to as green or sustainable finance. Sometimes these terms are used interchangeably given the strong linkages between the two, but they are not the same (Figure 3.2). The term "greening finance" adds further potential for confusion:

- *Sustainable finance* is a broader concept that incorporates the three aspects of sustainable development – economic, social, and environmental factors – into finance. Thus, it incorporates ESG (Environmental, Social and Governance) principles to evaluate companies and investments.
- *Green finance* is a subset of the wider sustainable finance category. It refers to the capital that funds projects that tackle climate and environmental problems, e.g. financing actions towards resource efficiency, sustainable agriculture, forestry, and waste and water management to address problems such as pollution, biodiversity loss, and climate change, more generally.
- *Greening finance* focuses on improving the management of financial risk related to climate and the environment (European Parliament, 2021[9]). This involves capital provided to companies that manage environmental risks more successfully, and thus are perceived as more environmentally friendly companies (European Commission, 2017[10]).

Figure 3.2. Links between sustainable and green finance

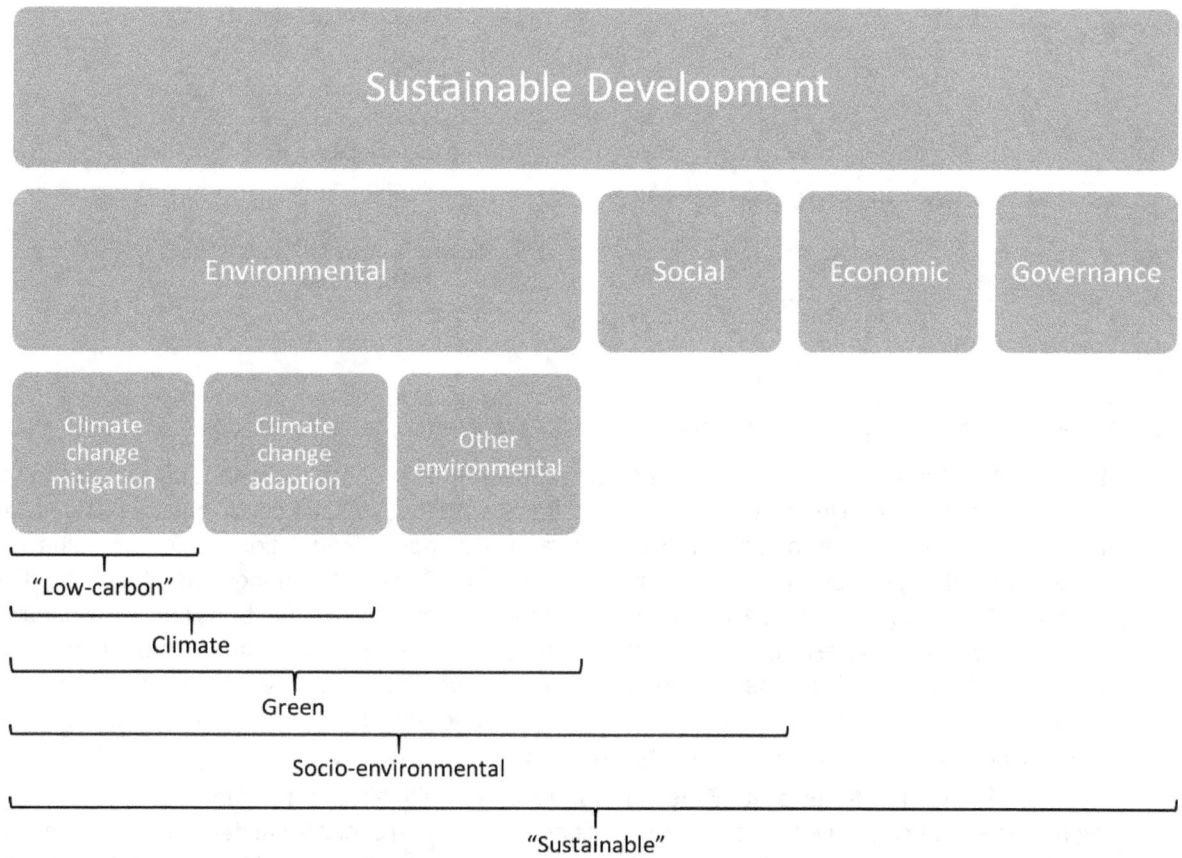

Source: (UNEP, 2016[11])

Green entrepreneurs often access financing from different sources at different stages of development (Figure 3.3). Early-stage innovation projects, notably climate technologies, typically rely on government funding or investment from large corporations. Governments can support early-stage projects directly (e.g. university research, subsidised R&D projects) and indirectly (e.g. providing financial support to networks, funding specialised training) (GFC, 2017[12]). Subsequently, as researchers and entrepreneurs begin to develop prototypes, private investment becomes important. Technology-based start-ups typically depend on venture capital (Bocken, 2015[13]) but business angel investment and more recently crowdfunding can also be important sources of funding (Wallmeroth, Wirtz and Groh, 2018[14]).

Figure 3.3. Sources of funding for climate technologies

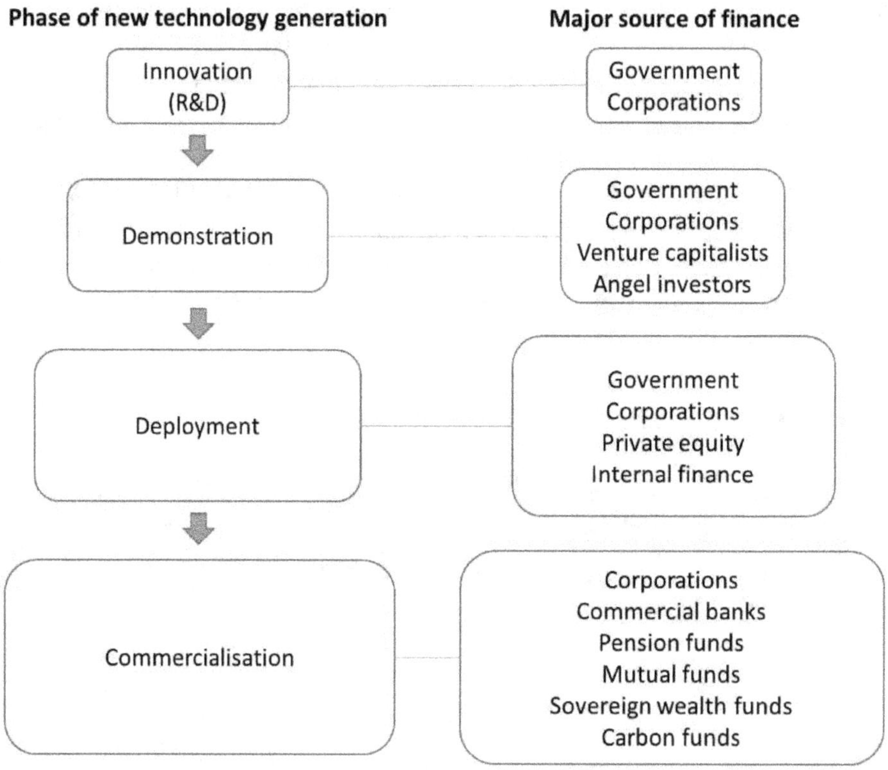

Phase of new technology generation	Major source of finance
Innovation (R&D)	Government, Corporations
Demonstration	Government, Corporations, Venture capitalists, Angel investors
Deployment	Government, Corporations, Private equity, Internal finance
Commercialisation	Corporations, Commercial banks, Pension funds, Mutual funds, Sovereign wealth funds, Carbon funds

Source: (United Nations, 2018[4])

There are several important actors in financial markets for green entrepreneurs:

- **Public sector and supranational regulators:** Governments at the national and supranational level have a critical role in setting the regulatory framework that sets the conditions for sustainable and green finance. This includes the EU's Green Taxonomy Regulation, which contains six environmental objectives: 1) climate change mitigation; 2) climate change adaptation; 3) the sustainable use and protection of water and marine resources; 4) the transition to a circular economy; 5) pollution prevention and control; and 6) the protection and restoration of biodiversity and ecosystem. In addition, the taxonomy sets three conditions that an economic activity has to meet to be considered as environmentally sustainable and thus it helps all actors transition to the EU's environmental objectives (European Commission, 2020[15]).

- **Public Financial Institutions (PFIs):** PFIs have a multi-faceted role in supporting green entrepreneurs through direct lending and investment, which can allocate capital to projects deemed too risky for private markets. They can also help to mobilise private capital through co-investment schemes and provide non-financial support to green entrepreneurs. For example, the European

Investment Bank (EIB) recently invested EUR 250 million in impact loans offered by Rabobank in the Netherlands to support sustainable entrepreneurs under favourable conditions (EIB, 2021[16]). Public banks are increasingly being mobilised to contribute to governments' sustainability and environmental goals.

In addition, COVID-19 recovery packages in many OECD countries expand sustainability and green financing for entrepreneurs (OECD, 2021[17]). For example, in the UK, GBP 11 million (EUR 13.2 million) was deployed in February 2021 to fund entrepreneurs through the Energy Entrepreneurs Fund (Gov.UK, 2021[18]).

- **Risk capital:** Equity investments are an important source of funding for green entrepreneurs. Many consider venture capital to be the most suitable form of finance for green start-ups but being green does not appear to increase the chances of receiving investments (Mrkajic, Murtinu and Scalera, 2017[19]). Although venture capital funding for climate technology declined in the United States in the first half of the 2010s (Gaddy et al., 2017[20]), there are signs that the global market has picked up in recent years. Industry estimates suggest that about USD 222 billion have been invested in climate tech between 2013 and the first half of 2021 and that year-over-year investment has grown 210% over this period (PWC, 2022[21]). Furthermore, the latest survey on venture capital funds and business angels (BA) by the European Investment Fund suggests that approximately 7 in 10 venture capital funds incorporate ESG criteria into their assessments, while 6 in 10 business angels do the same (EIF, 2020[22]). This shows a growing sensibility to sustainable and green finance in this market.
- **Debt markets:** The role of debt markets in the green financing arena has grown since the issuance of the first green bond by the EIB and the World Bank in 2007. Since then, the cumulative issuance of the global green bond market reached USD 754 billion as of 2019, with 5 931 deals (Climate Bonds Initiative, 2019[23]).
- **Impact investors:** Impact investing is an investment strategy seeking to generate positive and measurable environmental and social impacts while gaining financial returns (EIF, 2020[22]). One of the most important priorities for impact investors is to tackle environmental challenges. Impact investors are an important potential source of early-stage funding for green entrepreneurs because they can provide debt, equity or equity hybrid financing that is adapted to the entrepreneurs' needs (UfM Secretariat, 2018[24]).
- **Fintech:** Fintech companies have emerged as a new source of funding for entrepreneurs, including for green projects. The emergence of technologies such as Blockchain, Machine Learning, the "Internet of things" (IoT) and Artificial Intelligence hold potential for creating opportunities for a more inclusive and decentralised financial system (UNEP, 2016[25]), but it must be recognised that there are also risks that this will focus capital flows to profit maximising activities.
- **Online alternative markets:** Crowdfunding and peer lending platforms have created new markets where entrepreneurs can access debt and equity. Data suggest that the number of alternative lenders that offer green investment opportunities is increasing. For example, the UK is becoming an important hub for green crowdfunding as green investing expands (Peer2Peer, 2020[26]).

Using public-private partnership models to create opportunities

Public-private sector collaborations hold great potential for leveraging the strengths of a range of actors to create new opportunities for green entrepreneurs. In practice, several different approaches can be taken. In the Netherlands, for example, the Netherlands Enterprise Agency operates the Green Deal, which funds initiatives that accelerate the transition towards a more sustainable economy. It is a joint initiative by the Dutch Ministries of Economic Affairs and Climate Policy, Infrastructure and Water Management, the Interior and Kingdom Relations, and Agriculture, Nature and Food Quality. Green Deals are a form of funding agreement that finance coalitions of private sector actors, civil society organisations and local and regional government. Deals typically last for about two to three years and focus on one or more of the following themes: energy, food, water, bio-based economy, biodiversity, circular economy, mobility, climate and construction. An evaluation of the 201 green deals agreed between 2011 and 2016 found positive impacts of the individually funded activities as well as a decrease in many structural barriers that accelerated green innovation more broadly (Green Deal, 2017[27]).

Another approach that is used in OECD countries is to facilitate collaborations through innovation labs. This model typically provides a combination of business incubation support with a strong emphasis on facilitating collaborations between government, sector organisations, large firms, researchers and entrepreneurs to identify challenges and potential solutions. Often, sector organisations and large firms have a role in identifying challenges that researchers and entrepreneurs seek to address. Innovation labs are often organised by sector and there is a strong focus on supporting sectors in becoming more green. The results of innovation labs can be positive (see Israel case study in Chapter 4) but there is a strong risk that large firms use these types of arrangements to externalise their own innovation operations. This calls for close monitoring of activities by government.

Increasing diversity in entrepreneurship through green entrepreneurship policy

Green entrepreneurship is key in facilitating the transition to a more sustainable economy. It is well documented that many groups, including women, young people and immigrants, are under-represented in entrepreneurship (OECD/European Commission, 2021[28]). Raising participation among these groups can be an effective way of supporting green entrepreneurship. Some under-represented groups have a particularly high level of concern regarding environmental issues, and may therefore have a greater propensity to engage in green entrepreneurial ventures if they are empowered to do so. For instance, in the Spring 2021 edition of the European Commission's Eurobarometer, 24% of those 15-24 years old listed the environment and climate change among the top two issues facing their country. This compares to a figure of 15% among those 40-54 years old.

Policy makers are taking steps to tap into the potential of young people in the field of green entrepreneurship. An example of this is the EU's Erasmus Plus programme, which has a project on entrepreneurship, youth and the environment. This project seeks to provide young people with the tools and skills necessary to start a green business, through the development of an e-learning platform and handbook and the identification of role models. Meanwhile, the Green Youth Network in South Africa provides entrepreneurship training to young people in order to assist them in entering the green economy.

Implementing local public initiatives

Local governments also have a strong role in promoting and supporting green entrepreneurship. Many green entrepreneurship projects are supported by cities in their move towards becoming more smart and sustainable. Cities and metropolitan areas drive economic growth, as they contribute to about 60% of global GDP, but they also account for about 70% of global carbon emissions and over 60% of resource use. Many cities are adopting ambitious targets. For instance, Prague has a commitment to reduce CO_2 emissions by 45% until 2030 and become CO_2 neutral by 2050. To reach these goals, the city developed strategies to improve its environment. These entailed tree planting activities, organising green events, fostering a circular economy and boosting sustainable mobility, thus creating opportunities for green entrepreneurs.

Local initiatives are often funded and supported by national governments and international initiatives. This includes direct support as well as other incentives for cities, including international recognition. For example, the European Commission launched the European Green Capital Award (EGCA) to reward local efforts to improve the environment. ECGA is given yearly to a particular European city. Previous winners include Stockholm, Hamburg, Vitoria-Gasteiz, Nantes, Copenhagen, Bristol, Ljubljana, Essen, Nijmegen, Oslo, Lisbon, Lahti and Grenoble.

The role of non-government actors

In addition to governments, the private and non-government sectors have a strong role in supporting green entrepreneurs. Many global companies and foundations partner with green entrepreneurs in working towards sustainability objectives. For example, the Ellen MacArthur Foundation funds innovative ideas and start-ups that contribute to growing the circular economy. Meanwhile, the World Wide Fund for Nature (WWF) works with entrepreneurs, corporations and individual citizens in a range of projects aimed at reducing CO_2 emissions.

Corporate and individual philanthropists are also a growing source of support for green entrepreneurs. At the UN COP21 conference, the so-called "Mission Innovation" was born, aimed at accelerating the Clean Energy Revolution. One of its many initiatives, also supported by Bill Gates and other investors, is "Breakthrough Energy", which finances innovations that may contribute to reaching a world with net-zero emissions. More recently, Jeff Bezos launched the Bezos Earth Fund, which is designed to combat the effects of climate change by issuing grants to scientists, activists and other organisations in their efforts to preserve the environment. The fund announced 16 initial recipients of support, who will receive USD 791 million of funding.

Building demand for green solutions

Political commitments to shift social attitudes

Governments have collectively made a number of political commitments at various levels to signal the need to change the way that societies operate in order to mitigate the risks of climate change. These high-level objectives also seek to guide future policy development and shift social attitudes, which are critical for creating favourable conditions for green entrepreneurship (Domańska, Żukowska and Zajkowski, 2018[29]). One of the overarching guiding frameworks is the United Nations' (UN) Sustainable Development Goals (SDGs). The 2030 Agenda for Sustainable Development, adopted by all of the UN Member States in 2015, provides a shared blueprint for policy development. At its core are the agreed 17 SDGs, with 169 associated targets, which are integrated and indivisible, and represent an urgent call for action. Several of the SDGs' commitments are directly related to tackling climate change, strengthening environmental policies and developing a more sustainable planet. Accomplishing these objectives will require strong engagements from citizens, governments and non-government actors, including contributions from green entrepreneurs and corresponding public policies to facilitate this.

At the European level, the new European Green Deal was introduced to guide the EU towards becoming the world's first climate-neutral continent. The European Green Deal includes a set of new measures to reduce net GHG emissions by at least 55% by 2030 relative to 1990 levels. These include the development of the first European Climate Law; the extension of the Emissions Trading System to cover the maritime sector and reduce the free allowances allocated to airlines over time; the introduction of a Carbon Border Tax; the definition and deployment of a strategy for green financing; the adoption of a Sustainable Europe Investment Plan; and the creation of a Just Transition Fund to ensure that certain groups are not left behind. The European Commission presented its plan to implement the Green Deal in July 2021 and man of these measures are expected to contribute to the promotion of green entrepreneurship through the creation of new markets and opportunities.

This is supported by a number of more specific action plans such as the EU Circular Economy Action Plan. The action plan aims to make sustainable products the norm in the EU. It targets how products are designed, promotes circular economy processes, encourages sustainable consumption, and aims to ensure that waste is prevented and that consumed resources are kept in the EU economy for as long as possible (European Commission, 2020[30]). The plan outlines 35 actions with an initial focus on sectors that use the most resources and where there is a high potential for circularity such as electronics and ICT, batteries and vehicles, packaging, plastics, textiles, construction and buildings, food, water and nutrients.

Another important initiative led by the President of the European Commission is the New European Bauhaus. This is an interdisciplinary initiative to make the Green Deal a positive, "touchable" experience. It is intended to facilitate the exchange of knowledge and to create interdisciplinary projects to build towards a sustainable future. The New European Bauhaus aims to shape societal thinking, behaviours, and markets around new ways of living and building, including also public procurement. Many of the actions supported through this initiative will stimulate green entrepreneurship.

Many OECD countries have adopted national action plans to work towards achieving sustainability goals. In the US, for example, a range of executive actions have been taken to promote and support clean energy, build modern and sustainable infrastructure and re-establish the President's Council of Advisors on Science and Technology. Similarly, most OECD countries have defined strong national sustainability agendas.

Developing new economic models such as the circular economy

New economic models such as the circular economy hold potential for generating positive impacts on the environment and creating new opportunities for entrepreneurs. The circular economy is based on three core principles: 1) design out waste and pollution; 2) keep products and materials in use; and 3) regenerate natural systems (OECD, 2020[31]). This economic model can have an important role in achieving environmental policy objectives by increasing the share of renewable energy and recyclable resources and reducing the use of raw materials, energy, water and land. Some estimates suggest that the circular economy could be worth as much as USD 700 billion in consumer good material savings globally (OECD, 2020[31]). There are clear opportunities here for green entrepreneurs to bring new products and processes to market. Many activities in the circular economy are labour intensive, so there is also substantial job creation potential attached to it.

Government support to green entrepreneurs in the circular economy is slowly growing, notably by facilitating access to finance. The most common approaches used by governments are the provision of loans and grants. In the EU, the EIB offers loans for large-scale projects and guarantee mechanisms for smaller projects to access financing through local banks. The European Fund for Strategic Investments also offers several financing instruments that support green entrepreneurs in circular economy projects such as InnovFin, which was launched in co-operation with the European Commission under Horizon 2020. It offers support under thematic financing initiatives until the end of 2022.

A number of national and regional governments offer financial support for circular economy projects. This includes loan schemes such as "*ICF EcoVerde*", which is offered through Catalonia's Finance Institute (*Institut Català de Finances*). Grants are also used by national and local governments, including for example the Finnish Ministry of Economic Affairs and Employment and the municipality of Valladolid, Spain. However, grant schemes tend to support circular economy projects broadly (e.g. education programmes for children, business associations) rather than supporting green entrepreneurs in business creation. Another financial instrument that governments can use is revolving funds, which allow for revenues to be reinvested in new projects. For example, the city of Amsterdam in Netherlands invested EUR 30 million in more than 65 projects related to climate, sustainability and air quality through the Amsterdam Climate and Energy Fund (ACEF) and the Sustainability Fund (OECD, 2020[31]). There are some examples of governments providing growth capital to green entrepreneurs in the circular economy so that they can scale their businesses. In the UK, the London Waste and Recycling Board operates a growth fund called the Circular Economy Business Support Programme, which supports SMEs in scaling their business.

Another important tool for governments in supporting green entrepreneurs in the circular economy is regulation. Several governments are using sector-specific regulations to remove restrictions on the use of recycled materials. This includes, for example, the easing of restrictions in the wind energy sector in the Netherlands in 2017 that prevented the reuse of plastic turbine blades. This plastic can now be used as an input in the car and ship industry (Ministry of Economic Affairs, 2017[32]; OECD, 2020[33]).

Many governments across the OECD are increasing awareness of the circular economy among entrepreneurs and SMEs. Common approaches include communication campaigns, notably through dedicated websites and events. Short training schemes for entrepreneurs are another tool used to raise awareness. These are commonly organised by local governments (e.g. Public Waste Agency of Flanders, Belgium) and chambers of commerce (e.g. Glasgow Chamber of Commerce, UK). A less common approach is to use ambassadors that promote the circular economy in companies, sector organisations and local authorities. This approach is adopted by the London Waste and Recycling Board in the UK (OECD, 2020[31]).

A critical tool used in many countries, including the Netherlands and Israel, is to create networks for material chains to help entrepreneurs identify opportunities. For example, in Tilburg, Netherlands, a network for the textile sector aims to facilitate exchanges between entrepreneurs, producers, retailers, educational institutes, local governments and banks. It is key to share experiences across experts in each sector (e.g. tourism, construction, waste, etc.) to have a better understanding of what can be done, where the gaps exist and how these can be overcome. A similar but slightly different approach is to create marketplaces for recycled materials. For example, the city of Austin, United States, operates a secondary materials marketplace where businesses can acquire recycled materials.

Expanding green public procurement

Governments are starting to use public procurement as a tool for creating green markets and supporting green entrepreneurs. The European Commission has defined green public procurement as "a process whereby public authorities seek to procure goods, services and works with a reduced environmental impact throughout their life cycle when compared to goods, services and works with the same primary function that would otherwise be procured" (European Commission, 2008[34]).

Green public procurement holds great potential for supporting green entrepreneurs. Public authorities spend approximately EUR 1.8 trillion annually, representing about 14% of the EU's GDP (European Commission, 2021[35]). For example, CO_2 emissions would be cut by 15 million tonnes per year if the whole EU adopted the same environmental criteria for lighting and office equipment as the City of Turku, Finland, which reduces electricity consumption by 50%. In addition to directly purchasing goods and services that reduce environmental impacts, governments can also influence markets through procurement. For example, public authorities can create incentives for entrepreneurs and industry to develop green technologies and products. This is particularly true in sectors such as public transportation and construction and health services, where public authorities account for the majority of purchases.

Despite the myriad of benefits of green procurement, governments continue to face a range of barriers to expanding the use of green procurement. These barriers include low levels of awareness among public authorities and a lack of political support. One of the main challenges is that public procurement typically uses cost as a dominant criterion for awarding contracts and green procurement is perceived as increasing costs. Moreover, public authorities often lack practical tools to implement environmental criteria in procurement processes and legal expertise to define environmental criteria.

A specific tool that some governments are using to facilitate green public procurement is eco-labelling. The use of eco-labels helps public authorities specify the technical needs of the products and services being purchased and verify compliance with these requirements. The use of third-party verification can also reduce time in assessing bids and boost the credibility of these processes. The EU is actively supporting national and regional authorities in green procurement by providing technical support and providing practical tools such as the Buying Green Handbook (European Commission, 2016[36]).

References

Bocken, N. (2015), "Sustainable venture capital – catalyst for sustainable start-up success?", *Journal of Cleaner Production*, Vol. 108, pp. 647-658, https://doi.org/10.1016/j.jclepro.2015.05.079. [13]

Climate Bonds Initiative (2019), *Green Bonds: Global State of the market*, https://www.climatebonds.net/files/reports/cbi_sotm_2019_vol1_04d.pdf. [23]

Climate-KIC (2014), *The Future of Cleantech, "Co-opetition" not competition: Key lessons and recommendations*, https://www.climate-kic.org/wp-content/uploads/2014/09/TheFutureOfCleantech.pdf (accessed on 12 December 2021). [5]

Consoli, D. et al. (2016), "Do green jobs differ from non-green jobs in terms of skills and human capital?", *Research Policy*, Vol. 45/5, pp. 1046-1060, https://doi.org/10.1016/j.respol.2016.02.007. [2]

Domańska, A., B. Żukowska and R. Zajkowski (2018), "Green Entrepreneurship as a Connector among Social, Environmental and Economic Pillars of Sustainable Development. Why Some Countries are More Agile?", *Problems of Sustainable Development*, Vol. 13/2, pp. 67-76. [29]

EIB (2021), *Netherlands: Rabobank and EIB - €500m extra funding for sustainable Dutch entrepreneurs*, https://www.eib.org/en/press/all/2021-329-rabobank-and-eib-eur500m-extra-funding-for-sustainable-dutch-entrepreneurs (accessed on 23 February 2022). [16]

EIF (2020), *ESG considerations in Venture Capital and Business Angel investment decisions*, https://www.eif.org/news_centre/publications/eif_working_paper_2020_63.pdf. [22]

European Commission (2021), *Green Public Procurement*, https://ec.europa.eu/environment/gpp/index_en.htm (accessed on 12 December 2021). [35]

European Commission (2020), "A New Circular Economy Action Plan: For a cleaner and more competitive Europe", *Communication from the Commission to the European Parliament, the Council, the European Economic and Social Committee and the Committee of the Regions*, Vol. COM(2020) 98 final, https://eur-lex.europa.eu/legal-content/EN/TXT/?qid=1583933814386&uri=COM:2020:98:FIN (accessed on 23 February 2022). [30]

European Commission (2020), *Taxonomy: Final report of the Technical Expert Group on Sustainable Finance*, https://ec.europa.eu/info/sites/info/files/business_economy_euro/banking_and_finance/documents/200309-sustainable-finance-teg-final-report-taxonomy_en.pdf. [15]

European Commission (2017), *Defining "green" in the context of green finance*, https://ec.europa.eu/environment/enveco/sustainable_finance/pdf/studies/Defining%20Green%20in%20green%20finance%20-%20final%20report%20published%20on%20eu%20website.pdf (accessed on 23 February 2022). [10]

European Commission (2016), *Buying Green Handbook*, https://ec.europa.eu/environment/gpp/buying_handbook_en.htm (accessed on 12 December 2021). [36]

European Commission (2008), *Public procurement for a better environment*, Communication from the Commission to the European Parliament, the Council, the European Economic and Social Committee and the Committee of the Regions, https://eur-lex.europa.eu/LexUriServ/LexUriServ.do?uri=COM:2008:0400:FIN:EN:PDF (accessed on 12 December 2021). [34]

European Parliament (2021), *Green and sustainable finance*, https://www.europarl.europa.eu/thinktank/en/document.html?reference=EPRS_BRI(2021)679081 (accessed on 23 February 2022). [9]

Fundación Biodiversidad (2022), *Red Emprendeverde*, https://www.redemprendeverde.es/ (accessed on 22 February 2022). [3]

Gaddy, B. et al. (2017), "Venture Capital and Cleantech: The wrong model for energy innovation", *Energy Policy*, Vol. 102, pp. 385-395, https://doi.org/10.1016/j.enpol.2016.12.035. [20]

GFC (2017), *Options for support for technology collaborative research and development*, https://www.greenclimate.fund/sites/default/files/document/gcf-b18-12.pdf (accessed on 12 December 2021). [12]

Gov.UK (2021), *£11 million boost for energy entrepreneurs to turn green dreams into reality*, https://www.gov.uk/government/news/11-million-boost-for-energy-entrepreneurs-to-turn-green-dreams-into-reality?mc_cid=a7cb419008&mc_eid=e63640a80e. [18]

Green Deal (2017), *Evaluation Green Deals KWINK 2016*, https://www.greendeals.nl/sites/default/files/2022-02/Evaluation%20Green%20Deals%20KWINK%202016-%20summary-%20EN.pdf (accessed on 22 February 2022). [27]

McDaniels, J. and N. Robins (2017), *MOBILIZING SUSTAINABLE FINANCE FOR SMALL AND MEDIUM SIZED ENTERPRISES*, https://www.cbd.int/financial/2017docs/unep-smefinance2017.pdf. [6]

Ministry of Economic Affairs (2017), *Better Regulation: Towards a Responsible Reduction in the Regulatory Burden 2012-2017*, https://www.government.nl/documents/reports/2017/08/22/better-regulation-towards-a-responsible-reduction-in-the-regulatory-burden-2012-2017 (accessed on 12 December 2021). [32]

Mrkajic, B., S. Murtinu and V. Scalera (2017), "Is green the new gold? Venture capital and green entrepreneurship", *Small Business Economics*, Vol. 52/4, pp. 929-950, https://doi.org/10.1007/s11187-017-9943-x. [19]

OECD (2021), "An in-depth analysis of one year of SME and entrepreneurship policy responses to COVID-19: Lessons learned for the path to recovery", *OECD SME and Entrepreneurship Papers*, No. 25, OECD Publishing, Paris, https://doi.org/10.1787/6407deee-en. [17]

OECD (2020), *The Circular Economy in Cities and Regions: Synthesis Report*, OECD Urban Studies, OECD Publishing, Paris, https://doi.org/10.1787/10ac6ae4-en. [31]

OECD (2020), *The Circular Economy in Groningen, the Netherlands*, OECD Urban Studies, OECD Publishing, Paris, https://doi.org/10.1787/e53348d4-en. [33]

OECD (2018), *Fostering the use of intangibles to strengthen SME access to finance*, https://www.oecd-ilibrary.org/docserver/729bf864-en.pdf?expires=1613995708&id=id&accname=ocid84004878&checksum=F7F2663DC592FCD53232DDC731212C5F. [7]

OECD (2013), *Green entrepreneurship, eco-innovation and SMEs*. [8]

OECD/Cedefop (2014), *Greener Skills and Jobs*, OECD Green Growth Studies, OECD Publishing, Paris, https://doi.org/10.1787/9789264208704-en. [1]

OECD/European Commission (2021), *The Missing Entrepreneurs 2021: Policies for Inclusive Entrepreneurship and Self-Employment*, OECD Publishing, Paris, https://doi.org/10.1787/71b7a9bb-en. [28]

Peer2Peer (2020), *Second community municipal investment goes live on Abundance*, https://www.p2pfinancenews.co.uk/2020/08/25/second-community-municipal-investment-goes-live-on-abundance/. [26]

PWC (2022), *State of Climate Tech 2021: Scaling breakthroughs for net zero*, State of Climate Tech 2021 Scaling breakthroughs for net zero, https://www.pwc.com/gx/en/services/sustainability/publications/state-of-climate-tech.html (accessed on 23 February 2022). [21]

UfM Secretariat (2018), *Enabling access to finance for green entrepreneurs in Southern Mediterranean countries*, https://ufmsecretariat.org/wp-content/uploads/2018/12/UfMSectorialReport_Access-to-financing-for-green-enterpreneurs.pdf. [24]

UNEP (2016), "Definitions and concepts", http://unepinquiry.org/wp-content/uploads/2016/09/1_Definitions_and_Concepts.pdf (accessed on 23 February 2022). [11]

UNEP (2016), *Fintech and Sustainable Development: Assessing the implications*, http://unepinquiry.org/wp-content/uploads/2016/12/Fintech_and_Sustainable_Development_Assessing_the_Implications_Summary.pdf. [25]

United Nations (2018), *Climate technology incubators and accelerators*, https://unfccc.int/ttclear/misc_/StaticFiles/gnwoerk_static/incubators_index/ee343309e8854ab783e0dcae3ec2cfa6/c172d2f388234bdbbe3dd9ae60e4d7e9.pdf (accessed on 12 December 2021). [4]

Wallmeroth, J., P. Wirtz and A. Groh (2018), "Venture Capital, Angel Financing, and Crowdfunding of Entrepreneurial Ventures: A Literature Review", *Foundations and Trends® in Entrepreneurship*, Vol. 14/1, pp. 1-129, https://doi.org/10.1561/0300000066. [14]

4 Policy approaches to stimulating and supporting green entrepreneurship in Canada, Germany and Israel

This chapter examines three case study countries – Canada, Germany and Israel – approach stimulating and supporting green entrepreneurship. Each of these countries has a particular relevance to the Danish context, and has been identified as a source of learning for Denmark as it seeks to build a hub for green entrepreneurship. This chapter analyses the direct policy measures that are in place to support green entrepreneurship in each of the case study countries, as well as the indirect policy measures that contribute to a business environment that is more conducive to green entrepreneurship.

Highlights

Canada

- **Context:** Canada's domestic market is much smaller than that of its neighbour (United States), similar to the way that Denmark is positioned within the much larger European Union (EU) market. Federal policy is framed in the "A Healthy Environment and a Healthy Economy" climate plan, which is complemented by provincial governments and non-government actors. Direct support is delivered by government and non-government actors, including a pipeline of funding offered through the Business Development Bank of Canada (BDC) and Sustainable Technology Development Canada.
- **Key success factors:**
  - **Tailored financing to support entrepreneurs:** The BDC has adopted a segment-based approach that targets businesses based on their size and growth trajectory.
  - **High reporting standards:** The Clean Technology Data Strategy recognises the importance of providing decision makers with high-quality data on the green economy.
  - **Pricing carbon:** The Carbon Pollution Price Schedule will provide a competitive advantage to entrepreneurs with low-carbon products and solutions.

Germany

- **Context:** Denmark and Germany's geographical proximity and cultural ties mean that there is an opportunity for mutual learning between policy makers on both sides of the border. The overall policy agenda is driven by the federal government with further actions delivered by state governments. Core public support for green entrepreneurs is delivered through KfW Capital, the German Energy Agency, the Borderstep Institute for Innovation and Sustainability and the German Federal Environmental Foundation.
- **Key success factors:**
  - **Linking green entrepreneurship policies with wider environmental objectives:** Public initiatives for the promotion of green entrepreneurship in Germany are well aligned with wider environmental objectives.
  - **Recognising the role of public procurement:** New public procurement regulations have the potential to accelerate the green transition and lift demand for green goods and services.

Israel

- **Context:** Israel is widely recognised as the "Start-up Nation" and a leader in innovation in a number of cleantech fields. As a country of comparable size to Denmark, Israel's success in fostering entrepreneurship yields many pertinent lessons for Denmark. Many of the direct supports to green entrepreneurs are delivered by the Israel Innovation Authority, but a number of ministries are also involved.
- **Key success factors:**
  - **Funding opportunities:** Key to Israel's thriving start-up ecosystem is its venture capital market, which rests alongside strong public investment.
  - **Co-operation between private and public entities:** Many of Israel's successful policy initiatives link private sector actors with the public sector.
  - **Fostering networks:** Public policies play an important role in building entrepreneurial ecosystems and innovative communities of knowledge.

Introduction

The three case study countries have been selected based on their relative success in fostering entrepreneurship, and in particular, green entrepreneurship. Table 4.1 presents data on a variety of indicators that are relevant to green entrepreneurship. All three of the case study countries, as well as Denmark itself, are among the world's top performers in at least some of these areas. For instance, the volume of venture capital funding in Israel is second only to Singapore on a per capita to basis (Glasner, 2021[1]). Meanwhile, Canada was ranked third in the world in terms of the ease of starting a business in the World Bank's 2020 Doing Business study.

Table 4.1. Green entrepreneurship indicators: Denmark vs. Canada, Germany and Israel

	Indicator	Denmark	Canada	Germany	Israel
Entrepreneurship indicators	Business birth rate (2018)	11.0%	7.9%[1]	8.0%	8.5%
	Share of early-stage entrepreneurs who agree/strongly agree that they always consider the environmental implications of decisions (2021)	-	72%	63%	49%
	Venture capital funding per capita (28/10/2020 – 28/10/2021)	USD 340	USD 271	USD 202	USD 959
	Score for ease of starting a business (2019)	92.7	98.2	83.7	94.1
	Share of 18-64 population who agree that successful entrepreneurs receive a high status (2020)	-	81.3%	81.8%	83.7%
Environmental indicators	2030 target for GHG emissions	70% below 1990 level	40-45% below 2005 level[2]	65% below 1990 level	27% below 2015 level[3]
	Price on carbon (2021)	USD 24-28	USD 32	USD 29	-
	Environmentally related tax revenue as a share of GDP (2019)	3.4%	1.1%	1.8%	2.6%
	Environmental science citations per 1 000 people (1996-2020)	176	87	42	38
	Renewable energy, sustainability and the environment citations per 1 000 people (1996-2020)	37	14	8	8
	Share of patents in environmental technologies (2018)	24%	10%	14%	6%
	Environmental Performance Index score	82.5	71.0	77.2	65.8

1. Data for Canada are only available for employer enterprises.
2. Equivalent to 21-28% below 1990 level.
3. Equivalent to 42% above 1990 level.
Sources: (OECD, 2022[2]), (Glasner, 2021[1]), (Global Entrepreneurship Monitor, 2021[3]), (Israel Bureau of Statistics, 2021[4]), (World Bank, 2019[5]), (Scimago JR, 2021[6]), (Environmental Performance Index, 2020[7])

Canada

Canada has a variety of policies and initiatives to promote green entrepreneurship, many of them under a multilevel governance framework. Environmental policy in Canada is led by the federal ministry of Environment and Climate Change. However, many other public actors have clear complementary roles. Innovation, Science and Economic Development Canada is the lead ministry for supporting environmental innovation and entrepreneurship. As the government supported bank dedicated to SMEs and entrepreneurs, the Business Development Bank of Canada (BDC) also plays a very important role in the green entrepreneurship ecosystem. This funding complements other initiatives, such as grants offered by

Sustainable Technology Development Canada (STDC), the Canada Clean Tech Fund, which aims to help green start-ups to scale up, and regional programmes such as the Alberta Energy Transition. Efforts are also being taken to co-ordinate the measures that are in place, for instance through the creation of the Clean Tech Hub for Canada.

Many of Canada's policy efforts to address climate change, including those related to green entrepreneurship, fall within the Pan-Canadian Framework on Clean Growth and Climate Change (PCF), which was developed with the provinces, territories and Indigenous peoples. Published in 2016, the PCF includes more than 50 concrete actions that cover all sectors of the Canadian economy. These measures aim to reduce emissions, build resilience to a changing climate and enable clean economic growth. While the PCF has a scope that extends beyond green entrepreneurship, one of its four pillars focuses on innovation and support for clean technology. A number of subsequent plans have been announced, including the recent "A Healthy Environment and a Healthy Economy" climate plan that outlines actions to reach net-zero emissions by 2050.

Overall, green entrepreneurship funding mechanisms and solutions are rather comprehensive and well established in Canada. The government has also established a public procurement policy that promotes the sourcing of green products. Additional efforts may be needed to facilitate a smooth transition from oil and gas economic activities to green economy activities. This in turn can help to reinforce citizen awareness and shift consumer preferences towards greener products, solutions and start-ups. It is also important for some Canadian green start-ups to move from being local to global leaders (Box 4.1), namely through the direction of funding towards specific unsolved challenges and the development of a national super cluster strategy.

Box 4.1. Example of a leading green start-up in Canada

A good flagship green start-up from Canada is Carbon Cure, which is headquartered in Halifax. It is based upon innovative CO_2 technology, which leads to the injection of carbon dioxide into concrete, where it is converted into a stable mineral product. This solution has already contributed to a reduction of 131 666 tonnes of CO_2. Carbon Cure was founded in 2012 by Robert Niven, with the target of achieving a 500 million tonne annual reduction of CO_2 emissions by 2030.

The remainder of this chapter maps the public policies and programmes that are in place in Canada to promote green entrepreneurship. This covers initiatives overseen by the following entities:

- The Business Development Bank of Canada (BDC)
- Sustainable Technology Development Canada (STDC)
- Other federal initiatives
- MaRS Cleantech

The above entities provide direct support to green entrepreneurs, although green entrepreneurship is not necessarily their sole or primary focus. Policies that indirectly support green entrepreneurs by creating an economic and regulatory landscape that allows them to thrive are also presented. The chapter concludes with the key success factors of the policy approach in Canada, as well as the challenges encountered.

Policy actions that directly support green entrepreneurship

1. Business Development Bank of Canada

As the financial institution devoted to Canadian entrepreneurs, the BDC plays a key role in the promotion of green entrepreneurship. It focuses on entrepreneurs whose profitable companies create value for society and meet high environmental, social and governance standards, thus helping to foster a prosperous, inclusive and green economy. The BDC's activities are guided by three main principles:

1. Increasing access and reach, particularly for under-served groups;
2. Driving SME competitiveness by providing the advice and capital needed for companies to increase productivity, innovate and expand, and;
3. Providing an excellent client experience, including through the use of digital technologies.

The BDC has a long history of supporting clients hit by climate related disasters. However, the greatest contribution that it is making towards achieving climate resilience is by supporting entrepreneurs whose innovations are aiding in the transition to a low-carbon economy. This is achieved through the following channels:

CleanTech Practice

The BDC's Cleantech Practice invests in globally competitive cleantech firms as they discover and commercialise ways to combat climate change and pollution. Through the Cleantech Practice, the BDC assists green entrepreneurs in meeting their capital intensive needs for scaling and accelerating growth.

The BDC offers equity and flexible financing to cleantech firms with:

- A commercially validated and IP-protected technology that demonstrates a positive environmental impact;
- Proven market traction with significant potential for revenue growth and commercial contracts;
- The ambition to scale beyond CAD100 million in annual revenue, and;
- A clear pathway to profitability.

For the fiscal year of 2020, the BDC's total commitments through the Cleantech Practice reached CAD 253 million. The BDC is therefore well on track to deliver its CAD 600 million commitment to help build globally competitive Canadian cleantech firms, which can ultimately foster a long-term, commercially sustainable cleantech industry that can attract significant private capital investment.

Venture Capital

BDC Capital backs innovative Canadian companies that are reinventing industries and making them more energy efficient. The BDC is an active investor, providing equity investment alongside expert guidance and trusted advice in order to help entrepreneurs to scale up their businesses. In the fiscal year of 2020, BDC's Venture Capital division received CAD 431 million from divestiture investments, compared to CAD 125 million in 2019. This is in line with the BDC's strategy of supporting the best performing Canadian companies with the technology and talent needed to assume leadership at the global level, leading to revolving funds that support green entrepreneurship.

B Corp Certification Process

The BDC helps Canadian companies to achieve B Corp certification, thus encouraging entrepreneurs to examine their companies' environmental, social and governance (ESG) performance, and the impact of their products or services. The B Corp certification process was built by entrepreneurs who believe that the purpose of a company goes beyond making profits and extends to creating social and environmental good. B Corp entrepreneurs are a global movement of people whose companies create local prosperity, strong community values and a sustainable environment, under a framework that includes the following stages:

- *Assessment*: a free, online and confidential assessment to benchmark the positive impacts of entrepreneurs' companies;

- *Comparison*: a snapshot of how the start-up compares to thousands of peers worldwide;
- *Improvement*: a customised improvement plan accompanied with best practices.

Business services

The BDC provides a range of business services to clients. Offers includes entrepreneurial skills development, support in development of business plans and the development of marketing plans, including the identification of unique selling points and potential new customers. In addition, individualised technical support can be offered and some business development services are offered freely and openly through the Entrepreneur's Learning Center (users must create an account).

Fostering inclusivity

Women, young people, ethnic minorities, and indigenous people have traditionally faced more challenges in becoming entrepreneurs and running and growing businesses in Canada. This is often due in large part to difficulties accessing finance. BDC helps entrepreneurs from these under-represented groups to reach their full entrepreneurial potential by supporting their access to finance, providing networking opportunities and partners, and also championing their stories.

New businesses and young entrepreneurs often have difficulty finding the capital and advice they need to launch and grow their projects. To support them, BDC has developed a partnership with Futurpreneur Canada, a national non-profit organisation that offers mentoring, financing and other business resources to young entrepreneurs. BDC and Futurpreneur work together to promote youth entrepreneurship and increase financing for young entrepreneurs (18 to 39 years old). Under the recently renewed co-lending agreement, Futurpreneur and BDC provide loans of up to CAD 60 000. Given the values and priorities of younger generations, supporting youth entrepreneurship is also an effective means of promoting green entrepreneurship.

2. Sustainable Development Technology Canada

Sustainable Development Technology Canada (SDTC) plays a considerable role in supporting the advancement of clean technologies in Canada. SDTC seeks to identify and fund Canadian companies that are developing technologies with the potential to deliver sizeable environmental and economic benefits. Since its formation in 2001, SDTC has invested more than CAD 1.38 billion in 460 Canadian companies. Grants are provided to entrepreneurs at multiple stages of development, from the development of emerging innovations to commercialisation and market leadership. Cleantech companies that receive SDTC funding also benefit from SDTC's knowledge of entrepreneurial support systems and its network of federal and provincial partners. The average grant size is CAD 3 million, which typically covers around 33% of the project's costs. There is also a requirement for 25% of the project costs to be covered by private investment and for 50% of the costs to be incurred within Canada.

3. Other federal initiatives

Impact Canada

Impact Canada is a government initiative designed to generate solutions for government departments. This is achieved through Impact Canada's challenge platform, where solutions to challenges identified by government departments are developed by a diverse range of actors. An outcomes-based approach is adopted, whereby innovators are rewarded based on the measurable results and improvements that their solutions yield. Within this programme, Natural Resources Canada launched a CAD 75 million clean technology stream. This stream comprised challenges in the areas of decarbonising aviation, modernising power grids, designing better batteries, reducing energy use in mining, increasing the participation of women in the clean technology sector and improving sustainability of indigenous and remote communities.

Clean Growth Hub

The Clean Growth Hub, co-led by Innovation, Science and Economic Development Canada and Natural Resources Canada, is a whole-of-government focal point for clean technology and a unique advisory service model dedicated to helping Canadian clean technology innovators and adopters identify and navigate federal programs and services most relevant to their needs. More than 2 300 clean technology stakeholders have sought this service since its launch in 2018. The Clean Growth Hub leverages the knowledge, expertise, and network of its 17 member departments and agencies to provide tailored advice, including on research, development and demonstration, scaling up, and exporting. It also enhances co-ordination among federal organisations in delivering clean tech programmes and strengthens federal capacity to track clean technology outcomes through the Clean Technology Data Strategy (see below).

Clean Technology Data Strategy

The Clean Technology Data Strategy (CTDS) was established in 2017, with the objective of providing up-to-date information on the economic, social and environmental contribution of the environmental and cleantech sectors in Canada. Under the strategy, Statistics Canada publish a number of data products, including:

1. The Environmental and Clean Technology Products Economic Account, which measures the economic impact of environmental and cleantech products in terms of GDP, exports, imports and employment. These data are broken down by province.
2. The Survey of Environmental Goods and Services, which estimates the production of environmental goods and services by industry.
3. The Environmental Protection Expenditures Survey, which monitors expenditures made by industry to protect the environment.

The data published under the CTDS are an important tool in monitoring Canada's progress in the green transition. They also allow for regional and industry comparisons, which can be used to inform priority areas for public support or intervention.

4. MaRS Cleantech

Another impactful component of Canada's green entrepreneurship ecosystem is MaRS, a private, not for profit incubator and innovation hub. Originally conceived to support health sector solutions in Canada, it has since expanded its focus areas. Indeed, MaRS is now engaged with over 200 cleantech start-ups at varying stages of maturity. MaRS aims to provide comprehensive support to green start-ups, including facilities, technology surveillance, market exploitation, funding, networking or any other needs related to a particular green venture. MaRS is selective in its intake, only accepting and engaging with companies when there is a match between a project's needs and the resources that MaRS can provide. Specific green entrepreneurship targets are also promoted, through nurturing projects with high potential to reduce GHG emissions. For instance, "Mission from MaRS" is a new programme aimed at supporting 10 Canadian start-ups, which are together expected to contribute to a reduction of over 41 megatons of GHG emissions by 2040.

MaRS works in close collaboration with the government, trade commissions and other entities in order to facilitate access to domestic and international markets for green start-ups, and to assist these companies in moving from pilot schemes to full-scale commercial activities. Overall, MaRS is believed to be the largest urban innovation hub in North America, occupying 1.5 million square feet and having helped over 1 400 Canadian science-based start-ups that employ over 17 000 people.

Policy actions that indirectly support green entrepreneurship

Environmental regulations and mitigation

Canada has made significant progress implementing measures to reduce emissions throughout the economy. These include the phasing out of coal-fired power generation by 2030, reducing methane emissions from the oil and gas sector, phasing down the use of hydrofluorocarbons, continuing to improve the emissions performance of vehicles, and introducing a clean fuel standard. Other measures include work to develop and adopt increasingly stringent building codes to reduce energy use, as well as initiatives to accelerate the uptake of zero emissions vehicles. New funding will support these mitigation activities, such as investments in clean and renewable power generation. For instance, the CAD 675 million Emissions Reduction Fund's Onshore Program is helping Canadian onshore oil and gas companies to invest in green solutions that aim to lower methane emissions.

Carbon pricing

A strength of the Canadian policy framework is its carbon pricing system. Since 2019, carbon pollution pricing systems have been in place throughout Canada. Provinces tailor the pricing systems to local needs while ensuring they comply with the minimum national stringency standards set by the federal government. The government has also released a schedule for future changes to the price of carbon, which will see the minimum price of carbon rise from CAD 65 per tonne of GHG emissions in 2023 to CAD 170 in 2030. The higher price of carbon will create an increased demand for green products and solutions, representing a major opportunity for green entrepreneurs. The pricing schedule will also encourage investment in the green entrepreneurship ecosystem by providing greater certainty about the viability of green enterprises in the medium to long term.

Net Zero Accelerator Initiative

The Net Zero Accelerator Initiative, which is part of the Strategic Innovation Fund, will provide up to CAD 8 billion in funding for projects that contribute to lowering Canada's GHG emissions. The focus is on projects that support the decarbonisation of large emitters, the development of clean technologies and the creation of a batteries ecosystem in Canada. However, it is important to note that the minimum contribution to projects is set at CAD 10 million, meaning that the initiative principally benefits large or established companies rather than green entrepreneurs.

Success factors for stimulating green entrepreneurship

The above mapping of Canada's green entrepreneurship ecosystem has highlighted the following key success factors:

- **Tailored financing support to entrepreneurs:** The BDC has adopted a segment-based approach that allows it to deepen its understanding of clients and develop more relevant and applicable solutions. Six distinct client segments have been identified based on the size and growth trajectory of the business, and each segment now benefits from an adapted operational model that tailors the relationship according to client needs.
- **High reporting standards:** The Clean Technology Data Strategy recognises the importance of providing policy makers and other stakeholders with high-quality and regular data on the green economy. The availability of this data can assist with progress monitoring and the design of policy interventions. Another example of Canada's high reporting standards is the publication of annual reports on the status of implementation of the Pan-Canadian Framework on Clean Growth and Climate Change.[1] These reports summarise the progress made along the four pillars of the framework and outline the policy programmes and interventions that are planned for the future.

- **Pricing carbon:** The policy framework in Canada is helping to develop an economy in which there is space for green entrepreneurship to flourish. For instance, the Carbon Pollution Price Schedule will see the price of carbon rise significantly and consistently from an already high base (World Bank, 2021[8]). The relatively high price of carbon provides a competitive edge to entrepreneurs with low-carbon products and solutions. Meanwhile, the price schedule sends a strong signal to investors that market conditions will become increasingly accommodating to green enterprises (OECD, 2016[9]), which can help today's green entrepreneurs better meet their financing needs. Studies on the impacts of carbon pricing schemes elsewhere show that these policies can also significantly increase innovation in low-carbon technologies (Calel and Dechezleprêtre, 2016[10]).
- **Inclusive entrepreneurship:** The BDC has created a wide range of programmes to increase participation in entrepreneurship among under-represented groups. These programmes include the Indigenous Growth Fund, the Black Innovation Fund, the Women in Technology Venture Fund, and the Supplier Diversity Programme. The BDC also established a partnership with Futurpreneur Canada, to encourage young entrepreneurs that would like to develop their green projects.
- **Consumer preferences are shifting:** Although price remains the most important purchasing criterion for Canadian consumers, there is a growing demand for green products. 68% of consumers aged 18 to 34 are willing to pay at least 5% more for eco-friendly products, while fewer than half (46%) of older consumers are willing to pay this premium. Consumers are more likely to be willing to pay more for greener appliances (31%), food (30%) and vehicles (29%). Meanwhile, three-quarters of consumers have a positive view of businesses that care about the environment, highlighting the role that environmentally sustainable practices can play in enhancing brand image.

Pitfalls and challenges to consider

Although Canada is home to a number of thriving green entrepreneurship ecosystems, there are some challenges and pitfalls that are useful to consider and be wary of in the Danish context:

- **Challenges of moving online:** E-commerce is changing the business environment for entrepreneurs, bringing with it both challenges and opportunities. The COVID-19 pandemic accelerated the trend towards e-commerce for business-to-consumer and business-to-business companies. BDC research finds that Canadian SMEs will have to improve their online presence to remain competitive, since only 46% of them are currently selling online. Moreover, close to a third of entrepreneurs who sell online say that this channel is less profitable than their traditional operations.
- **Labour shortages:** Before the COVID-19 pandemic, many entrepreneurs and SMEs were having difficulty finding workers, a reflection of Canada's ageing population. The large baby-boom generation is heading to retirement, and there are fewer young Canadians to replace them in the workforce. As the economy improves, entrepreneurs and green entrepreneurs will once again be faced with recruiting difficulties in the years to come.
- **Challenge of adopting new technologies**: Big data, artificial intelligence, machine learning, robotics and the internet of things are redefining business models in all sectors. These technologies offer opportunities to reduce costs, increase efficiency, innovate and expand to new markets. However, they are also challenging to implement, namely due to the investments and expertise needed.

Germany

Climate change is a major issue in Germany, which is reflected by the array of public and private initiatives that are in place to support the green transition, many of which relate specifically to fostering green entrepreneurship. Germany also has a number of large industrial companies with well-established sustainability practices, providing opportunities for green entrepreneurs within their supply chains. The provision of venture capital and incubation is already being pursued by major German companies. For instance, BASF has had a venture capital arm since 2011. Another example is Next47, a venture capital fund founded by Siemens in 2016 that provides innovative start-ups with investment, acceleration and access to customers and networks. In 2021, Volkswagen also announced that it would be establishing a EUR 300 million venture capital fund to invest in decarbonisation start-ups.

The policies, initiatives and programmes developed in Germany are helping green entrepreneurs to establish themselves and grow. Indeed, Germany is home to 276 climate tech start-ups, a number which compares to 180 in the UK, 103 in France and 44 in Denmark (Speedinvest, 2021[8]). Moreover, the 2021 Green Start-up Monitor (GSM), established by the Borderstep Institute for Innovation and Sustainability and the German Start-ups Association together with the University of Duisburg-Essen and PwC Germany, finds that 30% of German start-ups can be classified as green, up from 26% in the 2018 GSM (Borderstep Institute, 2021[9]). Green start-ups therefore play a key role as engines of structural change in Germany, and they are well placed to be pioneers in bringing environmental innovations to the market. In areas such as energy storage and green hydrogen, German start-ups are among the world's leaders (Box 4.2). More broadly, Germany's share of the environmental and efficiency technologies market is three times its share of global economic output, highlighting once more the importance of green entrepreneurship for the German economy. Going forwards, maintaining certainty and stability with regards to green policies will be important in facilitating private sector investments. Also key will be efforts to bolster demand for green products across all segments of the German population.

> **Box 4.2. Example of a leading green start-up in Germany**
>
> A good example of a flagship German green start-up is Lilium, which is developing innovative electric-powered air vehicles, with headquarters and manufacturing facilities located in Munich. It aims to build radically better ways of moving, leading to a revolution in sustainable high-speed regional air transportation. With the ambition to become a global leader in air mobility, it was founded in 2015 and now has over 700 employees, who are working to make electric flights a reality, by developing the first electric vertical take-off and landing jet. The launch of commercial operations is expected to take place by 2024.

This chapter maps the public policies and programmes that are in place in Germany to promote green entrepreneurship. This includes initiatives organised by the following entities:

- The German Federal Environmental Foundation (DBU)
- KfW Capital
- The German Energy Agency (Dena)
- Other federal initiatives
- The Borderstep Institute for Innovation and Sustainability

It is important to note that while these entities' activities provide direct support to green entrepreneurs, green entrepreneurship is not necessarily their sole or primary focus. Policy actions that indirectly support green entrepreneurship are also described, after which the key success factors and challenges associated with Germany's policy approach to stimulating green entrepreneurship are presented.

Policy actions that directly support green entrepreneurship

1. German Federal Environmental Foundation

The German Federal Environmental Foundation (DBU) supports the transition to a sustainable economy by funding innovative and solution-oriented projects that contribute to the protection of the environment. Since 1991, DBU has supported more than 10 300 projects with EUR 1.9 billion of funding.

The DBU's Green Start-up Programme supports green start-ups with innovative and economically viable solutions to environmental challenges. Funding of up to EUR 125 000 per project is provided in the form of a non-repayable grant. The approval rate for the programme is approximately 7%, and in 2021, 14 new green start-ups received funding. One of the programme's main goals is to strengthen green start-ups in their role in the development of the green economy through innovative funding approaches. Support is provided to established start-ups as well as to start-up projects that have not yet been formally founded. Innovative spin-offs or start-ups created from an existing employment relationship, as well as university graduates and individuals with a suitable background or training are also welcomed. The programme aims to make green start-ups in Germany more visible and improve networking within the green start-up community by promoting suitable means of communication and providing information tailored to target groups.

The DBU also supports fathers and mothers who are involved in a new company, through the option of part-time founding. Through these support schemes, start-ups can be created during parental leave, and entrepreneurs are allowed to work up to 30 hours a week. Some of these start-ups are green start-ups.

2. KfW Capital

The public sector plays a significant role in bolstering Germany's venture capital industry, which is an important source of funding for entrepreneurs. An important player in this space is KfW Capital. With the support of the European Recovery Program (ERP) Special Fund, KfW Capital provides funding to start-ups by investing in German and European venture capital and venture debt funds. The level of investment of the ERP Venture Capital Fund Investment Programme in a particular fund is capped at EUR 25 million, or 20% of the fund's capital. KfW Capital, along with the Federal Ministry for Economic Affairs and Climate Action and a number of private investors, is a major investor in the High-Tech Gründerfonds (HTGF), which has a volume of around EUR 900 million and has invested in more than 650 high-tech start-ups since 2005. KfW Capital, the ERP Special Fund and the European Investment Bank also fund Coparion, which is a venture capital fund with a fund size of EUR 275 million. Coparion invests alongside private investors, with a requirement that these private investors commit the same funds and on the same terms and conditions.

The Future Fund is a new German umbrella equity fund with several financing instruments for technologies of the future. KfW Capital is responsible for co-ordinating the Future Fund. In 2021, the Federal Government provided an additional EUR 10 billion for the Future Fund, for an investment period up to 2030. Together with private investors, it is anticipated that more than EUR 30 billion of venture capital for start-ups will be made available through the Future Fund. The Future Fund is comprised of a variety of distinct components, including:

- **The DeepTech Future Fund (DTTF):** The DTTF is a new fund that will invest in German high-tech companies during their rapid growth phase, alongside private investors. EUR 1 billion has been made available over the next 10 years. The DTTF is managed by the High-Tech Gründerfonds (HTGF), potentially focusing – among others – on a number of industries related to green entrepreneurship including e-mobility and new energy.
- **The European Recovery Programme (ERP) / Future Fund Growth Facility:** EUR 2.5 billion has been made available by 2030 for KFW Capital to invest up to EUR 50 million in German and

European venture capital funds in order to enable larger and more frequent financing rounds for start-ups.

- **The German Future Fund / European Investment Fund (EIF) Growth Facility:** EUR 3.5 billion has been allocated within this facility for the period until 2030 to invest in growth funds and growth financing rounds for start-ups.

Sustainability is an important consideration for KfW Capital, as reflected in its Sustainability Policy (KfW Capital, 2021[13]) and its Exclusion List (KfW Capital, 2021[14]).[2] The wider KfW Group has also developed an innovative approach to monitoring the impact of its activities, by mapping its financial commitments to each of the 17 Sustainable Development Goals (SDGs). This indicates that in 2020, KfW made EUR 40.5 billion worth of new financial commitments that contributed to the Affordable and Clean Energy SDG, which compares to a figure of EUR 26.4 billion the previous year. Meanwhile, KfW's new financial commitments contributing to the Climate Action SDG rose from EUR 28.2 billion in 2019 to EUR 43.2 billion in 2020.

3. German Energy Agency

The Start Up Energy Transition (SET) is a platform run by the German Energy Agency (Dena) and the World Energy Council. SET seeks to stimulate innovation in the transition to cleaner energy sources. The SET Hub supports start-ups in developing innovative solutions that contribute to the energy transition, through the provision of education, training, mentoring and networks. A key element of this support is the SET Network Online Platform, which connects the more than 1 700 start-ups in its network with an array of investors, researchers, corporations, accelerators and public sector organisations involved in the energy innovation ecosystem.

4. Other federal initiatives

Micro-mezzanine Fund (*Mikromezzaninfonds Deutschland*)

The Micro-mezzanine Fund (MMF), which was established by the Federal Ministry for Economic Affairs and Climate Action, provides equity funding to start-ups, micro businesses and small businesses of up to EUR 50 000 per company, in the form of dormant equity holdings with a term of 10 years. Enterprises with a focus on environmental responsibility are particularly targeted by the MMF, and can therefore receive financing of up to EUR 150 000 per company. Other targeted groups are social enterprises, companies that were founded by unemployed people, and companies that are run by women or people with a migration background.[3] The Fund is co-financed by the European Social Fund and the European Recovery Program (ERP) Special Fund. Through the MMF II, which was set up in 2016 following MMF I, EUR 153 million can be issued to companies.

Business Meets Climate Action forum

Between 2017 and 2020, the Federal Ministry for the Environment, Nature Conservation and Nuclear Safety hosted the "Business meets Climate Action" forum, which allowed entrepreneurs to network on matters related with climate action.

5. Borderstep Institute for Innovation and Sustainability

The Borderstep Institute for Innovation and Sustainability is an independent research institute with a focus on green innovation, sustainable entrepreneurship, climate change and smart energy systems. It conducts publicly-funded research projects and also initiates collaborative projects with businesses, universities and trade associations.

Green Start-Up Investment Alliance

The Green Start-Up Investment Alliance, which is co-ordinated by the Borderstep Institute for Innovation and Sustainability, aims to support business angels and other early investors involved in the field of green enterprises. Criteria for assessing the sustainability of entrepreneurial ventures were developed for this purpose, in addition to transparent, reliable classifications of green start-ups. This initiative also provides high-quality matching services between green start-ups and investors. It is aiming to develop a permanent online offer for start-up financing in the green economy and to stimulate innovative financing opportunities for green start-ups, by facilitating the pooling of small investors in investor syndicates. Furthermore, the alliance plans to devise and test a monitoring instrument to record developments achieved in the field of start-up financing in the green economy.

StartGreen

StartGreen is an online information and networking portal for green start-ups in Germany, facilitating the exchange of knowledge and experience and the formation of partnerships. Members of the network gain access to the StartGreen newsletter and are also able to publish material on the platform and reach out to other network members. In order to celebrate and raise the visibility of innovative start-ups in the field climate protection and sustainability, StartGreen issues annual awards to standout companies in particular areas. StartGreen is funded by the National Climate Initiative and the Federal Ministry for the Environment, Nature Conservation, Building and Nuclear Safety, and is operated by the Borderstep Institute for Innovation and Sustainability.

StartGreen originated from the Startup4Climate initiative, which ran between 2013 and 2017. Startup4Climate was organised by the Borderstep Institute for Innovation and Sustainability, ADT, the German Association of Innovation, Technology and Business Incubation Centres, and the University of Duisburg-Essen, with the aim of increasing the proportion of green start-ups in Germany. It focused on start-up activities that could both open up new economic opportunities and create the basis for a new, long-term approach to reducing greenhouse gas emissions (GHG). The project compiled best practices in the field of green start-up investment and also offered direct support to new green businesses.

Policy actions that indirectly support green entrepreneurship

Climate Action Programme 2030 and Climate Change Act

In October 2019, the Federal Government of Germany agreed on the Climate Action Programme 2030, which was followed by the Climate Change Act in December 2019. While the Climate Action Programme 2030 pursues a comprehensive, three-pronged approach comprising regulatory law, price incentives and financial support, the Climate Change Act provides the legal framework for achieving Germany's climate targets. The two instruments are complementary and intended to help Germany achieve its climate target of reducing GHG emissions by 65% relative to 1990 levels by 2030.

Both of these programmes follow the guiding principle of enabling Germany to comply with its climate targets in an economically sustainable and socially equitable manner. The measures assumed pave the way for climate-friendly behaviour and climate-friendly investments. The federal government will provide EUR 54 billion between 2020 and 2023 to implement the initiatives established in the Climate Action Programme 2030. The projects funded span a broad spectrum of climate action activities, such as the National Climate Initiative, aimed to help cities, municipalities and districts to draw up climate action concepts or manage their energy supply and demand. Taking into account national targets for lowering emissions, it includes annual emission reduction targets for individual business sectors in the period between 2020 and 2030. In the energy sector, greenhouse gas emissions are to be reduced by 62% compared with 1990, in the buildings sector by 67%, in the transport sector by 42%, in the industrial sector by 51%, and in the agricultural sector by 36%. The German Climate Action Report 2019 shows that Germany is still about 4% short of achieving the 2020 target, largely because of higher emissions in the transport and buildings sectors. However, the report also indicates that Germany is getting significantly closer to achieving the climate target for 2020 than had previously been expected.

Renewable Energy Sources Act

Germany's Renewable Energy Sources Act came into force in 2021. Through this, Germany has adopted the target of significantly increasing the share of renewable sources in its energy production. In 2019, about 43% of electricity was generated from renewable sources, including wind and solar power, due in part to the wide range of state assistance made available. Germany is phasing out the use of coal to generate electricity. It is also aiming to refurbish more buildings to enhance energy efficiency, and is forging ahead with climate-friendly mobility. By 2030, the aim is for renewables to account for 65% of gross electricity consumption and by 2050 all electricity generation and consumption should be GHG-neutral. The electricity grids are being developed to ensure that green power can be used nationwide.

Energy Efficiency and Climate Protection Networks

The formation of networks for green entrepreneurs is another area of focus in Germany. Dena co-ordinates the Energy Efficiency and Climate Protection Networks (EEKN) initiative. The initiative was extended in 2021 to include climate protection. These networks are typically comprised of 5-20 members, which can include companies of any size, sector or geography. Their aim is to establish targets and implementation plans to enhance energy efficiency and climate protection measures among the participants. In order to facilitate a successful exchange, the network activities are supported by experts, including operators, moderators and energy consultants. This support is provided throughout the running time of the networks, which is usually between two and three years. Currently, there are over 350 EEKNs across Germany. Between 2021 and 2025, Dena plans to establish up to 350 new networks, with a goal of achieving a 5 to 6 million tonne reduction in GHG emissions through the measures implemented by network members.

Public Procurement

General Administrative Regulation for the procurement of climate friendly services (AVV Klima)

Each year, public procurement in Germany amounts to EUR 350 billion. The AVV Klima, which has been in force since 1st January 2022, introduces more stringent requirements in the area of sustainable public procurement. This recognises the important role that public procurement can play in driving demand for green solutions. AVV Klima stipulates that preference be given to climate-friendly options and that publicly procured products or services meet the highest possible energy efficiency class. Moreover, where possible, forecasts of lifecycle greenhouse gas emissions caused by the procured goods and services must be developed. AVV Klima also contains a list of products and services that are not permitted for public procurement on health or environmental grounds.

Competence Centre for Sustainable Procurement

The Competence Centre for Sustainable Procurement (KNB) is situated within the Procurement Office of the Federal Ministry of the Interior, Building and Community. The KNB provides training, information and education on sustainable procurement, acting as a central point of contact for federal departments, states, municipalities and other public procurement offices.

Success factors in stimulating green entrepreneurship

The above mapping of Germany's green entrepreneurship ecosystem has highlighted the following key success factors:

- **Linking green entrepreneurship policies with wider environmental objectives:** Public initiatives for the promotion of green entrepreneurship in Germany are well aligned with wider environmental objectives. For instance, the funding areas of the Green Startup Programme of the DBU are informed by the United Nations' Sustainable Development Goals (SDG), while KFW maps its financial commitments to the SDGs. These practices help to promote coherence between different green entrepreneurship initiatives.
- **Recognising the role of public procurement:** The new public procurement regulations that came into force in January 2022 require decision makers to take concrete steps to ensure that their purchasing decisions are as climate friendly as possible. These bold policy measures have the potential to accelerate the green transition and raise demand for goods and services provided by green entrepreneurs in Germany.
- **Recognition of economic and environmental goals within firms:** According to the Green Start-up Monitor, almost nine out of ten green start-ups attribute an important role to profitability in their current corporate strategy, and three out of four green start-ups rate the corporate strategy of "achieving a high market share" as being important (Borderstep Institute, 2020[15]). While all green start-ups in the dataset attach great strategic importance to their social and environmental impact, this is true for only two out of three of other start-ups. This difference becomes even clearer when it comes to converting the sustainability strategy into concrete management guidelines. Indeed, while all green start-ups integrate social and environmental impact into their key performance indicators, this is true for only 23% of the other start-ups.
- **Supporting staff development, motivation and participation:** For two-thirds of the green start-ups covered by the Green Start-up Monitor's analysis, strengthening the development and motivation of employees is also considered to be important, compared with just half for the other start-ups (Borderstep Institute, 2020[15]). Green start-ups more frequently adopt the approach of involving not only selected groups (such as top managers) but all employees in decision-making. This much stronger emphasis on the motivation, development and participation of their team members indicates that green start-ups not only pursue a positive external impact with their products and services, but also integrate ecological and social sustainability internally within their corporate culture and policies. The results of the Green Start-up Monitor also show that this philosophy has a positive effect on the human resource planning and recruitment of green start-ups.

Pitfalls and challenges to consider

It is useful to be aware of the following challenges that exist within Germany's green entrepreneurship ecosystem, which also offer lessons for other contexts:

- **Finance gaps:** Current entrepreneurship funding policies in Germany do not yet fully reflect the "double dividend" that green entrepreneurs provide by supporting economic and sustainability goals. Green entrepreneurs cannot fulfil their potential without suitable funding mechanisms in place, which is a particular challenge given the risk-averse nature of large investors in Germany (Borderstep Institute, 2020[15]). In fact, a major problem in Germany seems to be cultural conflicts between green founders and investors. Green entrepreneurs are often profit and growth oriented, but the economic metrics that investors look at are not the only deciding factor for green entrepreneurship. Green start-ups do not always expect a quick profit, since working sustainably may also mean slower growth, and therefore sometimes they are perceived by investors as being risky. As a result, very innovative green growth companies with a high potential to exert positive economic, social and environmental impacts cannot always exploit this potential due to a somewhat limited access to important seed and growth funding.

- **The need for recognition:** The lack of awareness of the importance of green start-ups in environmental and economic policies has limited the role that green start-ups are playing as a transformation engine for Germany. Up to now, green start-ups are working under the shadow of the digitisation and IT start-up landscape, and have not been recognised as an independent group that is critical for the sustainable development of Germany.

Israel

Israel is widely recognised as the "Start-up Nation", with one of the world's most developed networks of venture capital funds. The country faces significant environmental challenges related to its small size, high population growth, geographical location and lack of natural water resources. These challenges have necessitated innovation, which has helped Israel to become a dominant actor in the cleantech field and a recognised leader in desalination and water recycling.

Israel is widely recognised as one of the most advanced countries in a number of technologies, including green technologies, with a considerable number of entrepreneurs who are developing state of the art solutions for supporting the green transition. Indeed, Israel has an estimated 637 climate tech start-ups and growth companies (Box 4.3), and the share of Israeli start-ups that are climate tech companies has increased from 3% in 2011 to nearly 10% in 2020 (Moise, Klar and Siegmann, 2021[10]).

Green entrepreneurs benefit from a strong start-up ecosystem in Israel, supported by a highly skilled workforce, a dynamic venture capital industry and a supportive policy environment. The Israel Innovation Authority is an important policy player in Israel's start-up ecosystem, through its role in developing a network of technological incubators and innovation labs and allocating funding to researchers and entrepreneurs. Further efforts may be needed to create additional awareness and make sustainability a higher priority factor in determining purchasing decisions. This can include the use of green public procurement policies, since these are still relatively under-developed and price often remains the predominant consideration. Green labelling can also play a role in influencing purchasing decisions across the wider economy.

Box 4.3. Example of a leading green start-up in Israel

A specific example of one promising green entrepreneurship start-up coming from Israel, which is also a finalist for the 2021 Quality Sustainability Award of the International Academy for Quality, is UBQ Materials. Based upon disruptive new technologies, protected by international patents, the UBQ material converts urban and landfill waste into the most climate-positive thermoplastic on the market. With headquarters in Israel, UBQ is already working at a global scale, with tremendous potential impacts and opportunities being explored and considered.

The remainder of this chapter provides a description of the green entrepreneurship policy landscape in Israel, covering policies and programmes administered by the following organisations:

- The Israel Innovation Authority
- The Switchers Support National Partnership of Israel
- The Israel Innovation Institute

While green entrepreneurship is not the sole or primary focus of the above entities, they each have programmes and/or initiatives that provide direct support to green entrepreneurs. Policy actions that support green entrepreneurs indirectly through their impact on the wider economic and regulatory environment are also analysed.

Policy actions that directly support green entrepreneurship

1. Israel Innovation Authority

The Israel Innovation Authority (IIA) is an independent publicly-funded agency that was created to provide a variety of practical tools and funding platforms aimed at effectively addressing the evolving needs of the national innovation ecosystems, actively collaborating with all sectors and ministries. The IIA's Start-up Division aims to provide support throughout the entire entrepreneurial journey, from the early development of ideas to global market commercialisation. Help to green entrepreneurs is provided across all types of environmentally friendly technologies, from renewable and alternative energy to environmental conservation and water management. In total between 2018 and 2020, the IIA has supported 290 climate tech start-ups with a total of USD 250 million of funding. A description of the key programmes operated by the IIA's Start-Up Division is provided below:

Technological Incubators

Israel runs a national network of technological incubators, managed by private entities, which support the establishment of start-ups as they transition from an idea to a commercial product. The programme aims to nurture initiatives with disruptive technologies that are still at early Technology Readiness Levels (TRL) and thus have difficulties in raising private capital, with public support helping to de-risk the companies. The support offered by the incubators includes a physical site and infrastructures, administrative services, technological and business guidance, legal advice and access to partners, as well as connections with investors or potential customers. In approved early stage disruptive start-ups, 85% of the budget is covered by public funds (for up to a maximum of ILS 3.5 million over two years) and 15% is financed by the private incubator operators. In 2020, 90 requests were submitted to the various incubator programmes, of which 80 were approved for total grants of ILS 151 million.

Joint government support for pilot programmes

In a range of selected fields, the IIA collaborates with government departments in order to provide Israeli tech companies with support for R&D or pilot programmes. For instance, the Support Program for Innovation in Environmental Protection aims to develop and apply innovative clean technologies that will lead to a reduction in the use of natural resources and/or GHG emissions and examine their feasibility at an industrial scale. It is intended to reach Israeli technology companies in the field of environmental protection, which receive financial support covering 20%-50% of the approved R&D expenditure, with special funding of 75% provided to projects with exceptional potential. In order to address the regulatory obstacles that green entrepreneurs can often encounter, regulatory assistance may also be provided by the Ministry of Environmental Protection for conducting pilot tests under a unique regulatory framework. Meanwhile, the Support Program for Innovation in Reducing Greenhouse Emissions, which is run by the IIA in collaboration with the Israel Investment Centre and the Ministry of Environmental Protection, provides extensive support for projects that involve the first-time application of Israeli technologies in the areas of energy efficiency and GHG reductions. The programme provides up to 40% of funding support for investments in relevant projects. In total, the various support programmes for innovation in selected fields have provided climate tech start-ups with USD 60 million in funding towards R&D and pilot testing between 2018 and 2020.

Innovation Labs

The Innovation Labs facilitate collaboration between industry and entrepreneurs. They are operated by leading corporations within a particular industry, providing start-ups with access to unique technological infrastructures, market insights, marketing channels and expertise. The IIA funds 33% of the setup costs (up to a maximum of ILS 4 million) and 50% of the operating costs (up to a maximum of ILS 500 000 per year) of the innovation labs. Meanwhile, entrepreneurs are provided with a grant of up to 85% of the approved budget, up to a maximum grant of ILS 1 million for the first year, which can be followed by a grant of up to 50% of the approved budget for a second year.

An example of an innovation lab that supports green entrepreneurs in Israel is the Environmental Sustainability Innovation Lab (ESIL), located in Haifa. It aims to accelerate the growth of start-ups that use commercially viable technological solutions that support the green transition, through the provision of financial assistance, technological infrastructure and marketing expertise. The lab was founded by the IIA and is operated with the support of three large companies: EDF Renewables, Bazan Group and Johnson Matthey. In order to "connect global needs with Israeli technology solutions", ESIL provides "a dynamic ecosystem delivering economically viable technology solutions that support a socially just transition to a NetZero world", by nurturing and accelerating green start-ups and "connecting industries looking for green technology solutions with Israeli sustainability tech entrepreneurs and start-ups developing innovative and disruptive solutions to environmental problems" (ESIL, 2022[17]). The challenges that ESIL wants to address through green entrepreneurship cover the following topics: clean energy production and storage; optimisation of production processes; energy streamlining; advanced materials and chemistries for energy transitions; pollution treatment; air pollution reduction; control, prevention and reduction of risks and hazards; monitoring of pollution treatment processes; development of green products; material recycling and sewage treatment. Services and support provided by ESIL include funding, facilities, pilots, expertise and business development support.

Ideation (Tnufa) Programme

The Ideation (Tnufa) programme is intended for fledgling entrepreneurs who are interested in formulating and advancing an innovative technological concept. The programme supports entrepreneurs in developing a proof of concept, thereby enabling them to raise private funding or recruit a business partner for further development. It is designed to fund activities that are directly linked to the development of new technologies, such as prototype development, intellectual property, business development and exhibition expenses. Grants of up to 85% of the approved budget are provided, with a maximum value of ILS 100 000 per year over a two year period. In 2020, 539 requests were submitted to the programme, of which 152 were approved for total grants of ILS 16 million.

Seed Programme

This programme, which began operating in 2021, is intended for start-ups in the seed stage that are developing technologies in fields with stringent regulation, an extended timeframe before implementation, or an evolving market. These conditions often apply to green entrepreneurs' technological innovations. Support is given to companies that have not raised more than ILS 3.5 million and that have already signed a memorandum of understanding with a venture capital investor who is potentially interested in investing in the start-up.

Entrepreneurial Incubators in the Periphery

This programme aims to promote the development of innovation systems, technological entrepreneurship and employment in Israel's geographical periphery, through collaboration between designated incubators and higher education institutions, students, entrepreneurs, and start-ups. This collaboration is achieved by research activities and the development and commercialisation of projects that utilise local initiatives and resources. As part of this initiative, a local project operating within an incubator will be entitled to a grant of 85% of the approved budget from the Israel Innovation Authority, for up to a maximum budget of ILS 1 million, with the possibility of supplementary funding being provided by the incubator.

Young entrepreneurship

The Israel Innovation Authority is working in conjunction with the Ministry of Education to promote an entrepreneurship programme that will encourage and educate young people in business, scientific and technological entrepreneurship. The participants in the programme will gain experience in developing knowledge and products while making use of infrastructures such as science centres and museums, as additional important partners of this joint effort.

2. Switchers Support National Partnership of Israel

Entrepreneurs and start-ups are key enablers of the green and circular economy business models needed for the transition towards sustainable consumption and production patterns. The Switchers Support National Partnership of Israel was established to support Israeli green and circular entrepreneurs. This partnership is led by the Entrepreneurship Centre at Tel Aviv University (TAU) and is implementing a green entrepreneurship programme in Israel.

In May 2021, applications were opened for green entrepreneurs to develop a set of business development methodologies that boost sustainability and the circular economy. Following the launch of this first call, the Israeli Switchers Support National Partnership, led by the SwitchMed local partner (Tel Aviv University), has selected 12 green business projects to complete this green entrepreneurship programme. In total, 18 green entrepreneurs, of which 10 are women, are participating in workshops to develop their sustainable business models.

3. The Israel Innovation Institute

In partnership with a number of government bodies, the Israel Innovation Institute supports Israeli entrepreneurs whose ventures are helping to address global challenges. It does this by building innovation ecosystems that comprise relevant start-ups, corporations, academics, investors, government bodies and regulators in a particular field. Through disseminating information and hosting a variety of events, competitions and workshops, these innovation ecosystems facilitate knowledge sharing, networking and collaboration. An example of an innovation ecosystem that supports green entrepreneurs in Israel is EcoMotion, which is made up of 12 000 members and 600 start-ups in the field of smart mobility. The Israel Innovation Institute also encourages intrapreneurship, by empowering innovation leaders within established organisations and leveraging its networks to connect researchers with large organisations.

Policy actions that indirectly support green entrepreneurship

National programmes to reduce pollution

In recent years, Israel has taken a stronger stance on environmental policy matters. By the end of 2016, Israel had ratified the Paris climate agreement. Earlier that year, the government approved an ILS 500 million national programme aimed at reducing GHG emissions and increasing energy efficiency. As part of the 2017-18 budget, ILS 260 million was also allocated to a two-year programme focused on reducing air pollution. A reduction in emissions intensity was reported by the Ministry of Environmental Protection in 2017, indicating some early success in these policy efforts.

Carbon Tax

In 2021, the Israel Tax Authority and the Ministries of Energy, Finance, Environmental Protection and Economy jointly announced that an escalating carbon tax will be applied between 2023 and 2028. The tax will be capped to ensure that consumers do not experience more than a 5% increase in electricity prices during the taxation period. This means that the impact of the carbon tax on consumers' behaviours will be more limited than in other countries that have introduced heftier carbon pricing schemes.

Natural Resource Efficiency and Environmental Innovation Programme

The National Resource Efficiency and Environmental Innovation Programme was introduced in 2018 by the Israeli government, with an annual budget for environmental projects of ILS 756 million, of which ILS 143 million is allocated to the circular economy. An additional ILS 15 million is available to assist those working on environmental innovation and resource efficiency.

National Action Plan for the Circular Economy

The Ministry of Economy has created a national action plan for the circular economy. The corresponding roadmap focuses on three industrial sectors that have the largest potential to become circular: construction and infrastructure, packaging, chemicals and pharmaceuticals. The support tools defined under this action plan are the creation of a circular economy knowledge and consulting centre, funding for circular projects, and a leadership programme.

Israel Resource Efficiency Centre

The Israel Resource Efficiency Centre (IREC) helps manufacturing plants to use raw materials more efficiently through the provision of training and webinars. IREC estimates that raw materials account for 50-80% of companies' production costs. IREC's methodology therefore allows companies to significantly reduce their costs and limit their exposure to volatile swings in input prices, while also delivering wider environmental benefits. The centre is funded by the Ministries of Economy and Industry, Environmental Protection and Finance. Following a surge in demand for IREC's services during the COVID-19 pandemic, which created further pressures for businesses to make efficient use of resources, IREC received an additional
ILS 8.3 million. This allowed it to assist over 60 factories in becoming more resource efficient. The Ministry of Economy and Industry also operates an industrial symbiosis project, which seeks to identify potential ways in which one business' waste can become another business' input. The ultimate goal of the project is to reduce the landfill generated in Israel. Other active measures already in place to support the move towards a circular economy are the Institute for Advanced Manufacturing, a Circular Economy Accelerator, and a Circle Plastics Consortium.

Success factors in stimulating green entrepreneurship

The above mapping of Israel's green entrepreneurship policy landscape has highlighted the following key success factors in Israel's approach to stimulating green entrepreneurship:

- **Access to risk capital:** Israel's thriving start-up ecosystem is strengthened by a flourishing venture capital market, which rests alongside strong public investment. In Israel, there are approximately 70 active venture capital funds, 14 of which are international. With the highest volume of venture capital funding per capita in the OECD, Israel is able to support and fund the creation and growth of innovative industries and green start-ups. Israel's venture capital industry was initiated by the Yozma programme, under which a number of public-private venture capital funds were established. Through offering a range of incentives, the Yozma programme was highly successful in attracting private investors to Israel, to the extent that the public sector's role in the venture capital industry shifted away from direct investments in companies and towards providing guidance and stimulating the involvement of private investors.

- **Co-operation between private and public entities:** In many of the initiatives described above, private players combine efforts with the public sector, which is seen as the most promising and efficient way to achieve the desired outcomes and impacts in Israel. A good illustration of this approach is the Environmental Sustainability Innovation Lab (ESIL) in Haifa. Experience in Israel also shows that bottom-up approaches to green entrepreneurship can be effective, thus letting the private sector and entrepreneurs guide the choices being made and the nature of the projects being supported. This is then combined with a small number of very selective large consortia aimed at addressing major challenges that are considered a national priority.

  As technologies get more mature in Israel, public support is gradually reduced and new areas of priority may be assumed, as happened with the phasing out of public support for water related solutions. There is now an ongoing interest in promoting cultured food products, where some future unicorns are expected to appear.

- **Fostering networks:** Another defining feature of the policy framework in Israel is the role of public policies in building innovative communities of knowledge and efficient ecosystems, where multiple symbiotic players are brought together in order to share experiences and create collaborative projects. For instance, the IIA has been proactive in fostering collaborations between entrepreneurs and larger corporations, in particular through the Innovation Labs programme. However, the success of these collaborations relies on the innovation lab operators having the venture creation skills necessary to support start-ups. Also critical is having an open innovation mindset, which involves a focus on future technological gaps rather than current gaps.

- **Supporting low-tech green entrepreneurs:** Although there is no doubt that Israel has strong ecosystems in place for the promotion of green entrepreneurship, there is a lack of specific support programmes for green entrepreneurs that do not have a strong technological component attached to their projects. To tackle this challenge, Israel is now involved in an international project, entitled SwitchMed, which aims to speed up the shift to sustainable consumption and production patterns in the Southern Mediterranean, notably through the promotion of the circular economy and green entrepreneurship that is not technologically focused.

- **Investment in R&D:** Israel invests 4.1% of its GDP in R&D, compared to an OECD average of 2%. This is particularly important since strong research is the engine that drives science-based and green entrepreneurship.

- **Workforce skills:** According to the World Economic Forum's 2017-18 Global Competitiveness Index, Israel has the sixth highest availability of scientists and engineers in the world (World Economic Forum, 2017[18]). The country also has one of the highest ratios of university degrees and academic publications per capita. The STEM focus in Israel is driving many green entrepreneurship projects and successful start-ups.

Pitfalls and challenges to consider

- **Funding obstacles:** Despite Israel's rich investment landscape, in a survey of nearly 200 Israeli climate tech companies, 72% cited access to capital as their main challenge (Moise, Klar and Siegmann, 2021[16]). 85% of companies surveyed were hardware-based businesses, which often require larger investments and longer development timelines. Indeed, two-thirds of 4-7 year old climate tech start-ups in Israel have fewer than 10 employees, which is a symptom of the long development phase and delayed growth often associated with start-ups in the field. These factors can inhibit access to venture capital for climate tech start-ups. Israel does not currently have a dedicated climate tech investment group, although Firstime Ventures did announce a USD 100 million fund dedicated to sustainable investments at United Nations Climate Change Conference in November 2021.

- **Policy co-ordination:** There is also room for improvement in better integrating many of the ongoing initiatives that exist in Israel, such as the cleantech and circular economy activities. As an example of progress in this area, the 2050 Zero Carbon Action Plan is managed by the Prime Minister's Office and involves points of contact across multiple ministries (such as Economy, Industry, Transportation, Energy, Environment or Housing).

Lessons from Canada, Germany and Israel in promoting green entrepreneurship

1. Integrated governance models tie the system together

Many policy actions put forward by public authorities in the case study countries are managed by a common effort that connects different authorities, ministries and public agencies. Developing high levels of co-operation between public entities for the promotion of green entrepreneurship is important because it enables a greater degree of policy coherence and effectiveness (OECD, 2021[19]). For example, some programmes in Israel are specifically targeted to solve concrete problems that the country is facing in the environment and entail a shared effort from different public entities. These include the Support Programme for Reducing Greenhouse Emissions and the Support Programme for Environmental Protection. Both of these programmes are operated jointly by the Israel Innovation Authority, the Israel Investment Centre, and the Ministry of Environmental Protection.

2. A "whole business" approach to support green entrepreneurship

The path to success for entrepreneurs requires significant efforts in a variety of different areas. The experiences in the three case study countries highlight the benefits of taking a "whole business" approach to supporting green entrepreneurs, notably the ability to respond to different needs as they arise. In Canada, the BDC adopts a segment-based approach that provides tailored support to entrepreneurs depending on the businesses' size and growth trajectory. Each segment benefits from an adapted operational model that modulates the relationship according to specific client needs. For instance, BDC Capital has an arm dedicated to businesses with an intellectual property (IP) portfolio, providing them with patient capital and guidance from experts with experience in funding companies with intangible assets. The DBU Programme in Germany also provides tailored information to different target groups. In Israel, the Ideation (Tnufa) programme is intended for fledgling entrepreneurs who are interested in formulating and advancing an innovative technological concept in the initial R&D stage, in preparation for proof-of-concept and/or construction of an initial prototype.

3. Green entrepreneurship is about cleantech but not only about cleantech

Businesses are generally classed as being either high-tech or low-tech based on the share of their annual turnover that they invest in research and development (Reboud, Mazzarol and Soutar, 2014[20]). High-tech green businesses are often referred to as cleantech businesses, therefore green entrepreneurship is typically associated cleantech businesses involved in the development of technologies, products and services that help to solve environmental problems. Entrepreneurs involved in these endeavours can benefit from being embedded within technological ecosystems and connected with financing partners, including venture capitalists. The cleantech industry is growing rapidly, with the sector's global market volume reaching EUR 4.6 trillion in 2021. Future prospects are also positive, with global revenues in environmental technology and resource efficiency set to reach EUR 9.4 trillion by 2030. Therefore, governments have invested in developing cleantech support programmes. For example, Germany identified its buildings and transport sectors as being the largest polluters in its economy and is seeking to use new technologies from the cleantech sector to improve sustainability in these areas. This has been encouraged through the provision of public support to green entrepreneurial projects that create solutions to these environmental challenges. In Canada, BDC created the dedicated Cleantech Practice, which invests in globally competitive cleantech firms.

Although high-tech green entrepreneurship (or cleantech) is rightly a focus for policy makers in the case study countries, it is also important to acknowledge the role that low-tech projects can play in achieving environmental objectives. Indeed, the definition of green entrepreneurship encompasses all individuals that pursue ideas and solutions that have the potential to deliver environmental improvements, regardless of whether their activities are technology intensive or not. Examples of low-tech green entrepreneurship include plant-based restaurants or consultants providing advice on the implementation of green solutions. It is important to ensure that public support schemes also address the needs and challenges of low-tech green entrepreneurs, to avoid a situation in which these businesses fall through the cracks. Examples of public projects that support low-tech green entrepreneurs are the SwitchMed project in Israel and the DBU's Green Startup Programme in Germany.

4. Development of strategic partnerships to advance green entrepreneurship

In each of the three case study countries, governments invest in building networks of public and private sector stakeholders to support green entrepreneurs. These networks are an invaluable resource for green entrepreneurs because they can offer knowledge, expertise, as well as access to funding and market opportunities. Government actions can play an important role in the development of strategic partnerships with business associations, private incubators, universities and other relevant stakeholders. In Canada, BDC uses its network of 100 business centres across the country to provide in-person services to entrepreneurs with more complex borrowing needs. At the same time, it collaborates with both private and public sector organisations to increase their outreach and to engage more actively with entrepreneurs who want to contribute to environmental goals. These partnerships create a more favourable environment for starting and growing a business. In Israel, the entrepreneurial programme in the periphery regions collaborates directly with designated incubators and higher education institutions to improve entrepreneurial support in the areas of research, business development, and commercialisation.

5. Overcoming funding gaps

Green entrepreneurs often face higher levels of difficulty in accessing finance for their environmental projects. This is due to a variety of factors including a more extended path to market, policy uncertainty and the capital-intensive nature of many environmental projects, which can deter business angels, venture capital funds or other financial investors from lending. All of the case study countries have identified and addressed this challenge, developing a range of initiatives to reinforce the financial support that is available to green entrepreneurial projects, particularly in the areas of clean technologies. In Canada, BDC created the Cleantech Practice, which invests in globally competitive cleantech firms as they discover and commercialise ways of combatting climate change and pollution. Many of BDC's financing options provide long-term funding with flexible repayment terms, alleviating some of the challenges encountered by green entrepreneurs in funding capital-intensive projects over extended periods of time. In Germany, the GreenUpInvest initiative aims to involve business angels and other early investors in the field of green start-ups. The Israel Innovation Authority's Seed Programme supports start-ups in areas with stringent regulation, while the Ideation Programme helps entrepreneurs to develop a technological proof-of-concept, which in turn assists them in raising private funding or finding a business partner for further development.

6. Green entrepreneurship policies go hand-in-hand with national climate goals

As seen in Canada, Germany and Israel, green entrepreneurship policies and initiatives are usually well-aligned with national strategies aimed at achieving climate goals. These include international efforts such as the UN's Sustainable Development Goals and the Paris Agreement. Supporting green entrepreneurs who are innovating in the transition to a low-carbon economy can directly contribute to the achievement of climate targets. As specific examples of this alignment, the funding areas of the Green Startup Special Programme of the German Federal Environmental Foundation are informed by the scientific findings on the Planetary Boundaries and the United Nations' SDGs. Still in Germany, the StartUp4Climate initiative focuses on the consistent alignment of start-up support systems with climate protection and sustainability goals. At the same time, Germany decided to boost its efforts on innovation and climate technologies directly linked to the sectors that may contribute the most to greenhouse gas emissions, such as buildings and transport. In Canada, BDC's measures are also well aligned with the United Nations' SDGs and support the objectives of the Paris Agreement for a cleaner, more sustainable future.

7. Inclusion of under-represented groups

Many groups are under-represented in the area of entrepreneurship such as women and youth (OECD/European Commission, 2021[11]) but there is potential to boost green entrepreneurship by involving more of these under-represented groups in entrepreneurship. There is some evidence that entrepreneurs from some of these population groups are more likely to be involved in green entrepreneurship such as youth and women. There are some examples of governments using dedicated schemes to tap into this potential for boosting green entrepreneurship. For example, the Israel Innovation Authority is involved with several programmes that seek to engage young citizens or those from the peripheral regions in the country's green transition. In Canada, BDC has created a wide range of programmes that boost inclusivity, such as the Indigenous Growth Fund, the Black Innovation Fund, the Women in Technology Venture Fund, and the Supplier Diversity Programme. To encourage young entrepreneurs that would like to develop their green projects, BDC also established a partnership with Futurpreneur Canada, a national non-profit organisation that supports young entrepreneurs.

References

Borderstep Institute (2021), *Green Startup Monitor 2021*. [9]

Borderstep Institute (2020), *Green Startup Monitor 2020*. [17]

Calel, R. and A. Dechezleprêtre (2016), "Environmental policy and directed technological change: Evidence from the european carbon market", *Review of Economics and Statistics*, Vol. 98/1, https://doi.org/10.1162/REST_a_00470. [14]

Environmental Performance Index (2020), *2020 EPI Results*, https://epi.yale.edu/epi-results/2020/component/epi (accessed on 24 February 2022). [7]

ESIL (2022), *Environmental Sustainability Innovation Lab*, https://esil.co.il/ (accessed on 25 February 2022). [18]

Glasner, J. (2021), *These Countries Have The Most Startup Investment For Their Size*, news.crunchbase.com, https://news.crunchbase.com/news/countries-most-startup-investment/ (accessed on 24 February 2022). [1]

Global Entrepreneurship Monitor (2021), *Global Entrepreneurship Monitor*, https://www.gemconsortium.org/data (accessed on 24 February 2022). [3]

Israel Bureau of Statistics (2021), *Business Demographics - Survivors and Movements 2020-2018*, https://www.cbs.gov.il/he/mediarelease/pages/2021/%D7%93%D7%9E%D7%95%D7%92%D7%A8%D7%A4%D7%99%D7%94-%D7%A9%D7%9C-%D7%A2%D7%A1%D7%A7%D7%99%D7%9D-%D7%A9%D7%A8%D7%99%D7%93%D7%95%D7%AA-%D7%95%D7%AA%D7%A0%D7%95%D7%A2%D7%95%D7%AA-%D7%A9%D7%9C-%D7%A2%D7%A1%D7%A7%D7%99%D7%9D-2020-2018.aspx (accessed on 24 February 2022). [4]

KfW Capital (2021), *Exclusion List of KfW Capital*, https://kfw-capital.de/wp-content/uploads/2021_12_Exclusion-List.pdf. [16]

KfW Capital (2021), *Sustainability Policy*, https://kfw-capital.de/wp-content/uploads/KfW-Capital-Sustainability-Policy-1.pdf. [15]

Moise, T., U. Klar and A. Siegmann (2021), *Israel's State of Climate Tech 2021*, Israel Innovation Authority & PLANETech. [10]

OECD (2022), *SDBS Business Demography Indicators*, https://stats.oecd.org/index.aspx?queryid=81074 (accessed on 24 February 2022). [2]

OECD (2021), *SME and entrepreneurship policy frameworks across OECD countries An OECD Strategy for SMEs and Entrepreneurship*, OECD. [20]

OECD (2016), *Effective Carbon Rates: Pricing CO2 through Taxes and Emissions Trading Systems*, OECD Publishing, Paris, https://doi.org/10.1787/9789264260115-en. [13]

OECD/European Commission (2021), *The Missing Entrepreneurs 2021: Policies for Inclusive Entrepreneurship and Self-Employment*, OECD Publishing, Paris, https://doi.org/10.1787/71b7a9bb-en. [11]

Reboud, S., T. Mazzarol and G. Soutar (2014), "Low-tech vs high-tech entrepreneurship: A study in France and Australia", *Journal of Innovation Economics & Management*, Vol. n°14/2, https://doi.org/10.3917/jie.014.0121. [21]

Scimago JR (2021), *Scimago Journal & Country Rank*, https://www.scimagojr.com/countryrank.php (accessed on 24 February 2022). [6]

Speedinvest (2021), *Speedinvest & Creandum Report: The Growth and Future of Climate Tech Startups in Europe*. [8]

Will, A. (2019), "The German statistical category "migration background": Historical roots, revisions and shortcomings", *Ethnicities*, Vol. 19/3, https://doi.org/10.1177/1468796819833437. [22]

World Bank (2021), *State and Trends of Carbon Pricing 2021*, World Bank, Washington, DC. [12]

World Bank (2019), *Doing Business Legacy*, https://www.worldbank.org/en/programs/business-enabling-environment/doing-business-legacy (accessed on 24 February 2022). [5]

World Economic Forum (2017), *Global Competitiveness Index*, https://reports.weforum.org/global-competitiveness-index-2017-2018/competitiveness-rankings/#series=EOSQ133 (accessed on 31 May 2022). [19]

Notes

[1] The last synthesis report was published in July 2020.

[2] The KfW Capital Sustainability Policy is not directly applicable to the German Future Fund / European Investment Fund Growth Facility, which is covered by the European Investment Fund's sustainability regulations.

[3] In Germany, people who were born without German citizenship as well as those with at least one parent who was born without German citizenship are classed as having a migration background (Will, 2019[22]).